REVELS STUDENT EDITIONS

THE SPANISH TRAGEDY
Thomas Kyd

Manchester University Press

REVELS STUDENT EDITIONS

Based on the highly respected Revels Plays, which provide a wide range of scholarly critical editions of plays by Shakespeare's contemporaries, the Revels Student Editions offer readable and competitively priced introductions, text and commentary designed to distil the erudition and insights of the Revels Plays, while focusing on matters of clarity and interpretation.

GENERAL EDITOR   David Bevington

Dekker/Rowley/Ford   *The Witch of Edmonton*
Ford   *'Tis Pity She's a Whore*
Jonson   *Volpone*   *Bartholomew Fair*
Kyd   *The Spanish Tragedy*
Marlowe   *The Jew of Malta*   *Tamburlaine the Great*
Marston   *The Malcontent*
Middleton/Rowley   *The Changeling*
Middleton or Tourneur   *The Revenger's Tragedy*
Webster   *The Duchess of Malfi*   *The White Devil*

Plays on women: An Anthology
Middleton   *A Chaste Maid in Cheapside*
Middleton/Dekker   *The Roaring Girl*
Anon.   *Arden of Faversham*
Heywood   *A Woman Killed with Kindness*

REVELS STUDENT EDITIONS

THE
SPANISH TRAGEDY
Thomas Kyd

edited by David Bevington

based on The Revels Plays edition
edited by Philip Edwards and published
by Manchester University Press, 1988

MANCHESTER
UNIVERSITY PRESS

Manchester and New York

distributed exclusively in the USA
by Palgrave

Introduction, critical apparatus, etc.,
© David Bevington 1996

Published by Manchester University Press
Oxford Road, Manchester M13 9NR, UK
and Room 400, 175 Fifth Avenue, New York, NY 10010, USA
http://www.manchesteruniversitypress.co.uk

Distributed exclusively in the USA by
Palgrave, 175 Fifth Avenue, New York, NY 10010, USA

Distributed exclusively in Canada by
UBC Press, University of British Columbia, 2029 West Mall,
Vancouver, BC, Canada V6T 1Z2

British Library Cataloguing-in-Publication Data
A catalogue record is available from the British Library

Library of Congress Cataloging-in-Publication Data
Kyd, Thomas, 1558–1594.
    The Spanish tragedy / Thomas Kyd; edited by David Bevington.
        p.   cm.—(Revels student editions)
    'Based on the Revels plays edition edited by Philip Edwards.'
    ISBN 0-7190-4344-1 (pbk.) (alk. paper)
    I. Bevington, David M.   II. Title,   III. Series.
PR2654.S6   1996
822'.3.dc20   95—21694

    ISBN 0 7190 4344 1 *paperback*

    First published 1996
    10 09 08 07   10 9 8 7 6

Printed in Great Britain
by Bell & Bain Ltd, Glasgow

Introduction

born in 1558 (yr Queen E. came to throw))

Despite its immense popularity in its own day, The Spanish Tragedy was not associated with the name of Thomas Kyd, in any document that has survived, until 1612, more than two decades after the play was written and produced. Kyd is none the less a likely person to have authored this play. Born in London in 1558 to a family of some standing, educated there at the highly esteemed Merchant Taylors' school though never in attendance at Oxford or Cambridge so far as is known, Kyd became an established professional dramatist. Francis Meres, Thomas Heywood and Thomas Dekker refer to his fame, his industry, and his being (in Meres's estimation) among 'our best for tragedy' (*Palladis Tamia*, 1598). Kyd seems to have been brought up in his father's trade as a scrivener or clerk-copyist, and may have been employed by Lord Strange (who was also Christopher Marlowe's patron) in a secretary-like capacity.

6 yrs older than Shakes. + Marlowe

copied legal documents

Kyd's credentials as a dramatist are thus not unlike Shakespeare's: a family of modest social status but comfortable means, no university education but excellent schooling with many years of Latin, and above all a practical education in the writing of plays through involvement in the burgeoning London theatres and in the life of the city itself. A disputed passage from Thomas Nashe's *Menaphon* seems to credit Kyd with having written an early and now-lost *Hamlet*, a play that no doubt featured, like Shakespeare's *Hamlet* and Kyd's *The Spanish Tragedy*, a revenge plot, ghosts, chorus figures, Senecan speeches of highly wrought passion, sensational murders, reflections on cosmic injustice, the dilemmas of choice between stoical passivity and violent action that the protagonist-revenger must somehow resolve, a love affair blighted by mayhem, and a play-within-the play. Kyd also translated *Cornelia* from the French of Robert Garnier (published 1595) and may possibly have written *Soliman and Perseda* (c. 1589–92), on the subject of the play-within-the-play in Act IV of *The Spanish Tragedy*. Another translation from Garnier, called *Portia*, is lost. Kyd's name is unconvincingly associated with four or five other plays of the 1580s and 1590s. He died in 1594, seemingly in a wretched state, having

1

*did not go to university (neither did S.) but still applied classical hallmark of humanism

Plays belonged to co. not the writer [handwritten annotation]

Solomon + Paseda [handwritten annotation]

play w/in a play [handwritten annotation]

suffered (unjustly, it seems) physical torture and disgrace for his alleged associations with the 'atheistical' Marlowe, with whom in fact he had shared rooms in which they did their writing.

The Spanish Tragedy may have been written and produced in about 1586 or 1587, or perhaps as late as 1590. It was published in 1592. During the years leading up to and after the Spanish Armada in 1588, English audiences might well have been fascinated by a representation of high tragedy in Spain and Portugal; the play does not allude to the Armada itself, but interest in Spain certainly continued unabated after that event. Names, events and places of recent Iberian history are suggestively implied in the play's dialogue, but without much precision. Spain had defeated Portugal in the bloody battle of Alcantara in 1580; Portugal was ruled after 1582 by a viceroy; Terceira, in the Azores, fell to the Spanish in 1583. *The Spanish Tragedy* begins with the defeat of the Portuguese viceroy, and alludes to Terceira at I.iii.82. A masque that Hieronimo stages to entertain the King of Spain and the Portuguese Ambassador alleges several instances in which English soldiers have played decisive roles in Iberian history, eliciting from the noble spectators on both sides an admission that indeed 'English warriors' have conquered both Spain and Portugal, 'And made them bow their knees to Albion' (I.iv.140–71). Kyd is not above catering to his audience's jingoistic faith in England's national superiority. Yet the supposed history, reaching back into the twelfth and fourteenth centuries, is a medley of inaccuracies, and the suggestions of contemporary relevance are vague. Kyd's chooses Iberia as a colourful and distant locale in which to set his fictional account of grand tragedy and revenge. Spain, like Italy, was a place about which English audiences might expect to hear a tale of nefarious intrigue and secret murder. The patriotic attitudes are highly relevant to 1586–90, but the play justifies itself as sensational entertainment without much recourse to contemporary history.

Although Kyd apparently followed no one source in writing *The Spanish Tragedy*, he certainly made use of the Roman dramatist Seneca. The French dramatist Robert Garnier, whose *Cornelia* and *Portia* Kyd translated into English, had shown how Seneca was to be adapted to the rigorously neoclassical demands of Renaissance aristocratic theatre. Like Seneca's plays, many of which were themselves adaptations of Greek tragedies by Sophocles and Euripides, Garnier wrote tragedies that followed the classical 'rules'. Events occur within a twenty-four-hour span of time, in a single location.

Marlowe + Kyd were roomies
*gay together? [handwritten annotation]

Violence takes place offstage and is reported by messengers or other witnesses. Long declamatory speeches in formal verse express the heightened emotional distress of the chief characters. The single action moves through exposition and complication to catastrophe and denouement in a formal classical structure prescribed by Aristotle, Quintilian and other writers on tragedy. No comedy is allowed to intrude on the rarefied atmosphere of tragedy, the most noble of the classical genres. Plots are generally taken from classical mythology or ancient Roman history. The cast of characters is relatively small. Significantly, such plays need not have been staged; Seneca's own plays were 'closet' dramas designed to be read by the discerning in an age of debased public spectacles. We do not know that Kyd's *Cornelia* was ever performed. He dedicated it to the Countess of Sussex, suggesting that he aspired to the courtly and intellectual circle of the Countess of Pembroke (who translated Garnier's *Marc-Antoine* in 1590 as a closet drama) and her brother, Sir Philip Sidney. Sidney was well known for his animadversions against romantic popular drama in his *Defence of Poesy*.

Fortunately for English drama, Kyd needed to write for a living. In *The Spanish Tragedy* he tempers his Senecan model with more popular forms of entertainment. The result is a rich and complex interaction of elite and popular elements that could prove chaotic at times in dramas written for the professional London stage but which had the potential for fulness and variety. Kyd's play is immensely theatrical in ways that Seneca and Garnier are not; his delight in spectacle revels in those very elements that Aristotle and Sidney had devalued in defining the criteria for great tragedy. Masques and dumb shows make for the kind of pageantry that English audiences had long enjoyed in courtly and popular entertainments. Scenes at the Spanish and Portuguese court provide occasion for sumptuous royal costuming and for processional entrances of ambassadors, courtiers, counsellors, torchbearers, servants, no doubt in as large numbers as the acting company could provide. A Portuguese subplot, about the villainous Villuppo's near success in supplanting the virtuous Alexandro in the Viceroy's affections, is tangentially related to the story of Prince Balthazar's captivity at the court of Spain, but exists mainly as a separate action designed to suggest edifying comparisons with the play's main story. Comic scenes, such as that in which Pedringano braves it out with the Hangman only to be hanged after all (III.vi), delight in double entendres and joking about death.

The play's structure, with four acts separated by choric interludes, bears a resemblance to classical and Senecan tragedy but in an idiosyncratic fashion (four acts instead of the prescribed five) that owes as much to medieval and Tudor drama, where didactic chorus figures are common, as to classical precedent. Onstage violence includes one sensational murder in Act II, a shooting and a hanging in Act III, a suicide early in Act IV, and a scene of catastrophe at the end in which the stage is littered with corpses. Stage properties designed for various executions are brought on to enrich the spectacle; at other times, the scene demands thrones, crowns, gloves, tables and chairs for a banquet, drinking cups, books, heraldic shields, a window, a mysterious box, a bloody handkerchief, pistols and other weapons, ropes, various letters or other documents, and still more. Musical instruments play for royal entrances, dead marches and the like. A 'discovery' effect brings a corpse into sudden view. Overhearings and use of disguise are common. Rather than contenting itself with a single location, the play makes a point of shifting in alternating scenes from Spain to Portugal and from the public world of the court to the private world of murderers and avengers. The duration of time is not precisely indicated, but would seem to require some fairly substantial delays (as in *Hamlet*) for the revenger to learn the truth and settle on a course of action.

The Spanish Tragedy is, then, a remarkable mix of classical (mainly Senecan) and native English dramatic materials, created for a London theatre that was beginning to enjoy enormous commercial success. The play burst upon the London scene at the beginning of, or shortly before, the remarkable decade of the 1590s, when Shakespeare's career was getting into full swing. Kyd's tragedy is more or less contemporaneous with the great plays of Marlowe's short career. Along with Marlowe's *Tamburlaine*, *The Spanish Tragedy* was one of the frequently revived and influential plays of its era. It was the acknowledged grandfather of the revenge play, a genre which enjoyed a tremendous vogue in such dramas as *Titus Andronicus* (c. 1589–92) and *Hamlet* (c. 1599–1601) by Shakespeare, *Hoffman, or A Revenge for a Father* (1602), by Henry Chettle, *The Revenger's Tragedy* (1606), perhaps by Thomas Middleton or Cyril Tourneur, *The Revenge of Bussy D'Ambois* (c. 1601–11) by George Chapman, and still others, along with many plays like John Webster's *The Duchess of Malfi* (1612–14) and Middleton and Rowley's *The Changeling* (1622) in which the revenge motif is part of a more complex tragic structure. Seldom do we find a play with such an extensive lineage as that of *The Spanish Tragedy*.

Part of the play's stunning appeal was, and continues to be, its vivid juxtaposition of romantic intrigue, sudden violent death and cosmic questioning about the nature of the human condition. To begin with the last of these, *The Spanish Tragedy* is notable for the presence onstage, throughout the entire action, of the Ghost of Don Andrea and his guide, Revenge. We begin with Andrea's remarkable account of his soul's journey to the underworld, immediately after he perished in a recent battle between Spain and Portugal. The heightened descriptions of the rivers of Hades where the boatman Charon and the guard-dog Cerberus stand duty, the deepest hell where murderers and adulterers suffer a variety of eternal punishments and the scene of judgement in which Andrea's eternal dwelling-place is determined, have no immediate function in the main plot of *The Spanish Tragedy*; they are here to establish a mood of tragic seriousness and even terror. The consequences of human action can be dire in this depiction of the afterlife: lovers and brave warriors sport in the Elysian Fields, while perjurers and usurers are scalded in boiling lead or choked with melting gold under the watchful eye of Furies with their whips of steel. The afterlife is thus a place of Dantesque justice and retribution. It is a pagan afterlife, presided over by Pluto and Proserpina; it rewards courtly virtues like valour and devoted service in love. Kyd's highflown poetry invests this afterlife with Gothic splendour and enchantment. In the theatre, we are vividly aware that the pagan gods are eternally present, and that human life is continually being measured in the context of that ethical system.

Andrea and Revenge 'sit and see' (I.i.90, III.xv.39) the play we witness with them, a tragedy about Spain. They speak only before, between and after the four acts of the main action. They call themselves a 'Chorus in this tragedy' (I.i.91), and the play proper is staged for them; in this sense, *The Spanish Tragedy* is itself a play within a play. Andrea and Revenge occupy a special theatrical space, somewhere metaphorically at least between us as audience and the players in the main action. The chorus figures interpret for us from their intermediate, timeless, eternal realm. Andrea especially is useful in pacing the audience's expectations. The opening Chorus establishes a mood of anticipation as Andrea and we are introduced to the court of Spain where we will learn of Prince Balthazar's interest in Bel-imperia. At the end of Act I, Andrea is furious to see things going so well for his enemies, Balthazar and Lorenzo. After Act II, with the murder of Andrea's dear friend Horatio and the discomfiture of his erstwhile love Bel-imperia, Andrea still demands impatiently to know if Revenge has only brought him hither 'to increase my pain'. By the end of Act III, during which, it appears, Revenge has dozed off for a while, Andrea bids him waken to quiet Andrea's uncontrollable alarm at what appears to be a cosy relationship that has developed between Hieronimo and Lorenzo, thus seeming to abort any hope for revenge. A dumb show of an intended wedding that is quenched with blood partly satisfies Andrea's hope for a gory ending after all, and so he consents to sit through the rest of the play. At the end, his expectations more than amply fulfilled, Andrea asks the privilege of sentencing his fallen enemies to their eternal torment.

The choruses thus serve the function of pacing our expectations as we, like Andrea, move from curiosity to impatience to puzzled horror and ultimately to clarification. The movement nicely describes the shape of tragedy, as defined by classical theorists, from exposition to complication and thus through the catastrophe to a violent kind of resolution. And if Andrea is our stand-in as the type of anxious spectator (though with a bias towards revenge that we do not necessarily share), Revenge is Kyd's master of ceremonies and presiding spirit. From the start, he knows the story of the play to come, as Andrea does not. He sets the scene, and assures Andrea that his worries are unfounded; despite the appearances that things are going well for Andrea's enemies, Revenge promises eventually to turn 'Their joys to pain, their bliss to misery' (I.v.9). Andrea is too impatient and cannot look sufficiently ahead: 'Thou talk'st of harvest when the corn is green' (II.vi.7). Revenge's onstage sleep is symbolic, we now realize: 'although he sleep awhile' (III.xv.23), Revenge is not in fact dead but is practising a ruse common to all revengers, that of biding his time. Revenge knows that Andrea is mistaken in supposing that Hieronimo is really in league with Lorenzo. Revenge's astute 'reading' of the text is instructive to us as audience, lest we mistake the appearance of Hieronimo's deceptive strategy. Revenge, then, is a more informed viewer than Andrea, because he is also the author and stage manager of this play. He it is that will direct his actors to strike at the right time and thereby bring to a close the demonstration of perfect revenge that this playwright-figure has prepared for his naive but involved spectator,

Andrea. The shape of Revenge's revenge is the shape of Kyd's tragedy.

When we move to the play itself that Andrea and Revenge and we are all watching, we find a structure very like that which the chorus figures describe for us, of growing complication and frustration leading eventually to release and clarification. Take, for example, the rivalry between Andrea and his enemies, Balthazar and Lorenzo. At first the relationship, though adversarial, appears to be gentlemanly and honourable. The General's account in I.ii of the just-completed fight between Spain and Portugal gives credit to both sides. Andrea attacked bravely; the Portuguese Prince Balthazar brought up reinforcements and in the ensuing mêlée slew Andrea; as Balthazar was 'insulting' (i.e. exulting insolently) over Andrea's dead body, Horatio joined the fray to avenge the death of his dear friend Andrea and overcame Balthazar (I.ii.65–80). Nothing could seem more heroic and noble. The Spanish King, on hearing this account, is ready to reward Heironimo's son Horatio with 'this battle's prize' (l. 97).

Yet a tussle soon breaks out between Horatio and Lorenzo as to which can claim Balthazar as prisoner. Horatio insists that he unhorsed the prince, while Lorenzo asserts he first seized the prince's weapon. Balthazar compounds the confusion by yielding himself to both (ll. 152–65). The King attempts to emulate the wisdom of Solomon by giving weapons and horse to Lorenzo and the ransom money to Horatio, but the quarrel refuses to go away. With each succeeding account of the death of Andrea, the more confused we are as to what actually happened. Was he killed in fair fight as it seemed at first, or was he overwhelmed by superior numbers? The latter impression of foul play is certainly endorsed by Bel-imperia, who asks rhetorically, in conversing with Horatio, 'what was't else but murd'rous cowardice, / So many to oppress one valiant knight / Without respect of honour in the fight?' (I.iv.73–5). The more we hear of the matter, the less it appears to smack of honour.

This increasingly dark view of martial action on the battlefield is compounded by the various men's relationship to Bel-imperia, daughter to the Duke of Castile and the King's niece. She is the centre of an increasingly bitter amorous intrigue. Andrea tells us right at first of his devotion to her as his lover: 'In secret I possessed a worthy dame, / Which hight sweet Bel-imperia by name' (I.i.10–11). Although the details of their clandestine affair are left vague, the subject keeps coming up as a cause of acrimony between Andrea and

Bel-imperia's family. Lorenzo lectures his sister, reminding her how 'I did shield thee from my father's wrath / For thy conveyance [i.e. underhand service] in Andrea's love, / For which thou wert adjudged to punishment' (II.i.46–8). Later, he again obliges her to remember 'that old disgrace / Which you for Don Andrea had endured'. Plainly, what aggravated the Duke of Castile is that his daughter was 'so meanly accompanied'—that is, involved in an affair with a man of distinctly lower rank than her own (III.x.54–7). The duke himself, when he thinks she has agreed to marry Balthazar, expansively insists that 'It is not now as when Andrea lived— / We have forgotten and forgiven that' (III.xiv.111–12). The patriarchal males of this proud royal family are not about to let Bel-imperia choose her own mate, in or out of marriage.

Their plan, of course, is to have Bel-imperia marry Balthazar and thereby become the means of uniting Spain and Portugal in one dynasty. International marriages of this sort were common in the Renaissance, and there is nothing inherently shocking about their desire to further political union in this way. The Spanish King favours the idea; lacking heirs himself, it would seem, he looks to his brother's family and especially his niece for 'the whole succeeding hope / That Spain expected after my decease' and that is dashed by the violent deaths of the play's final scene (IV.iv.203–4). Lorenzo stands to gain from the marriage by the political power that will accrue to one so closely allied to the king-to-be and his bride. Only Bel-imperia's wilfulness stands in the way of a political and dynastic triumph.

From her point of view, on the other hand, the whole thing smells of coercion and corrupt influence. She knows the villainous mind of her brother Lorenzo, and, even if her father is a more decent man, he is, in her view, duped and misled. More seriously still, Bel-imperia's dilemma casts a whole new light (for us and for Andrea as audience) on the question of Andrea's defeat and death in war. Bel-imperia suspects foul play in the use of superior numbers to overwhelm one warrior on the field of battle, but the iniquity may go deeper than that. Is it a coincidence only that Balthazar and his troops ganged up on Andrea and that Lorenzo then moved in on Horatio's capture of Balthazar, claiming the prince for himself? The play invites us to wonder if a conspiracy preceded the battle, and that the death of Andrea was all choreographed by Lorenzo and perhaps his family as a means of taking Bel-imperia away from the hated Andrea and bestowing her on the man who has killed Andrea.

This 'reading' of the plot has the advantage of explaining how Andrea's desire for revenge is central to a play in which the main business of the revenger, Hieronimo, is to seek compensation for the death of his son, Horatio. The reading is not certain—that is, we cannot be sure that a conspiracy preceded the battle. Yet the play invites such a reading, and thereby begins to indicate how wild and unpredictable a thing revenge can be.

Horatio's relationship to Andrea and Bel-imperia is one of the play's most arresting features. As friend of the slain warrior, Horatio immediately assumes his friend's role as lover of Bel-imperia. Their courtship is an astonishing amalgam of calculation and passion. Surely Bel-imperia takes on Horatio as her lover, in part at least, as a way of staving off the demands of her family for her to marry Balthazar; she can see what is coming long before they propose the marriage to her. The new love affair is her defiant answer to her father's and brother's anger at her having given herself to a man of lower social rank. Quite possibly she is responding to what she perceives in Lorenzo to be a kind of sexual jealousy bordering on incestuous desire; Lorenzo is glad to have her possessed by a man he calls his best friend and alter ego, but not by men he cannot control. Bel-imperia gibes at oppressive male authority in her family, preferring amorous encounters where she is on a more equal footing or in fact superior in social station. Her love duel with Horatio (II.iv) is one of the most ardently erotic scenes in Renaissance drama, and all the more compelling because it reaches its climax in Horatio's grisly death by hanging. Love and death: word games of military-amorous encounter culminate in an orgasm of onstage violence. Horatio for his part is drawn to the match by his remembrance of the dead Andrea; nothing seems more suitable to him than to replace his friend in the arms of Andrea's erstwhile lover. Andrea, for his part, watches all this from the sidelines with no hint of disapproval; his only concern is that Bel-imperia should not give herself to Balthazar. Motives of revenge produce strange bedfellows, as it were.

Once Horatio is dead, the focus of the play shifts increasingly to his father, Hieronimo. It is he who finds the body, mourns in the company of his wife Isabella, and must then seek some means of revenge. He anticipates Hamlet as the man of probity upon whom is placed the burden of revenge and for whom that grave responsibility serves as a challenge to ideas of human and divine justice. Hieronimo must figure out just what has happened and what it all means. Like Hamlet, he faces a cunning enemy of high social rank whose skill in deception makes the task of discovering the truth and responding to it all the more difficult. Like Andrea, too, Hieronimo must 'read' the action he witnesses for signals of divine intent, and must pass through a long phase of growing doubt and despair before the answer is made clear.

At first, the gods seem to smile on Hieronimo. He is Spain's Knight Marshal, and his brave son is honoured by the King with recognition of his martial achievements. Hieronimo's pride in Horatio is touching; the son's victory in battle confirms a father's dearest hopes. 'That was my son', he boasts to the King as Horatio marches by with the army,

> Of whom, though from his tender infancy
> My loving thoughts did never hope but well,
> He never pleased his father's eyes till now,
> Nor filled my heart with overcloying joys.   (I.ii.117–20)

When Hieronimo argues on behalf of Horatio's right to a reward for his brave services done, the King responds by awarding Horatio the privilege of enjoying Balthazar's ransom money. The father, meantime, is accorded the privilege of presenting a masque before the King and the Portuguese ambassador extolling Spain's might over her enemies. The heavens and the earthly kingdom seem bent on doing honour to Hieronimo and his son.

Such good fortune makes all the more appalling Hieronimo's sudden discovery of his son's corpse hanging in the arbour of the family garden. Nothing prepares the father for this shock, and his response is accordingly disoriented. He seems unable to recognize the body at first, and goes on to experience a clinical case of denial. Vows of revenge seem at first easy, but time brings doubt. The terrible event at the centre of his consciousness appears to challenge all meaning in life: 'O world, no world, but mass of public wrongs, / Confused and filled with murder and misdeeds!' (III.ii. 3–4). Like Hamlet, Hieronimo generalizes philosophically from the basis of his predicament. The issue poses a test to the heavens themselves:

> O sacred heavens, if this unhallowed deed,
> If this inhuman and barbarous attempt,
> If this incomparable murder thus
> Of mine, but now no more, my son
> Shall unrevealed and unrevengèd pass,

How should we term your dealings to be just,
If you unjustly deal with those that in your justice trust?

(III.ii.5–11)

Just when he is most adrift in his own uncertainty, Hieronimo
happens on a letter that falls as though from heaven. Is it heaven's
will indeed? The letter, from Bel-imperia in her place of confinement, informs him that the murderers of his son are Lorenzo and
Balthazar. Is Hieronimo now free to act? His first response, like
Hamlet's upon hearing from his father's ghost the identity of his
murderer, is to 'swoop to my revenge'; the second thought is to
exercise caution. Is this a trap? Can Hieronimo be certain? Lorenzo
and his family are dangerous enemies. Like Hamlet, accordingly,
Hieronimo resolves to 'try / What I can gather to confirm this writ'
by 'circumstances', by evidence (III.ii.48–9). He assumes a guise of
madness to throw off his enemies, though his own emotional distress
is so great that we as audience have difficulty in sorting out the
pretended from the real. In his own office as Knight Marshal he tries
cases that are like his own in testing the validity of justice, dispensing
to others the fairness and equity that he cannot obtain for himself
(III.xiii). The cunning and political power of his enemies drive
him to a private revenge that goes against the creed of his own
judicial career. In Hamlet-like soliloquies he ponders the as-yet-
unperformed duty of revenge and the torment that his soul must
meanwhile endure (see for example III.vii.1–18). Those who do not
know him well conclude from his ravings and odd behaviour that he
is 'passing lunatic' (III.xi.32). Like Hamlet he considers and then
rejects suicide (III.xii.19). He issues a direct indictment of Lorenzo
in a public assembly, putting his adversary on notice as does
Hamlet, but takes cover in his seeming madness when the King
and others severely question his behaviour. He is torn between
promptings for revenge and a Stoical faith in the quiet life of renunciation (III.xiii.1–44). He thinks he sees his son's ghost come
from the underworld 'To ask for justice in this upper earth' (ll. 133–
4).

These extensive similarities to Hamlet's dilemma can be put to
several critical uses. They underscore the indebtedness that Shakespeare owed to Kyd, and help define the genre of the revenge play as
it came to be practised on the Elizabethan stage. At the same time,
they open up a consideration of the crucial ways in which Hieronimo

is not a simple model for Hamlet. However much Hieronimo may feel the pull of reluctance in his task of revenging his son's death, he becomes increasingly hardened and violent in accomplishing what he must do. Whereas Hamlet almost stumbles on his final best chance to kill Claudius as a consequence of a duel with Laertes and various plots of poison that Hamlet knew nothing about, so that his final act of killing the king is almost unpremeditated and prompted by self-defence, Hieronimo proceeds to his last rendezvous as the agent of death in a deliberate manner. Kyd's model here is perhaps Seneca's *Thyestes*, in which the revenger dupes his enemy into devouring his own children. (Shakespeare used a similar story in his first tragedy, *Titus Andronicus*.) Hieronimo grows more cunning as the play's catastrophe approaches. He becomes a schemer, no longer appealing to the heavens but instead throwing off suspicion with his protestations of mad innocence, making insincere offers of friendship to Lorenzo and the rest that are convincing enough to fool Andrea (III.xiv.156–61, III.xv.15–16), and the like. Revenge to Hieronimo is now a simple moral issue, endorsed by the gods themselves. 'I see that heaven applies our drift', he tells Bel-imperia, 'And all the saints do sit soliciting / For vengeance on those cursèd murderers' (IV.i.32–3). Bel-imperia joins his conspiracy by confirming his crafty lies to Lorenzo and Balthazar, thereby entrapping them into taking on their fatal roles in 'Soliman and Perseda'. Hieronimo becomes almost a grimly comic character as he assures them that he will not endanger their dignity by playing in a tragedy; Nero offers a precedent (ll. 87–9). Nero! The young men ought to be warned simply by the name. Instead, they march to their fate in a plot of entrapment that is at least as much ironic in tone as tragic. As a consequence, Hieronimo becomes an ironic revenger, bloody, determined, victorious.

The Spanish Tragedy thus ends as a savage triumph for revenge in its most nakedly pagan aspect. This is true not simply for Hieronimo and Bel-imperia, but for Andrea and Revenge as spectator-chorus. When Andrea, in a frenzy of blood-lust, demands and gets the authority to provide everlasting judgement for his enemies, his sentences lacks any hint of mercy. The Duke of Castile, for all his well-meaning attempts in the play to find out the dark truth of his son Lorenzo's perfidies and to provide well for his daughter, is to have his liver torn at perpetually by vultures. With his demise and that of his family go all hopes of political union between Spain and Portugal, a cause that in worldly terms would seem to have much in its favour. The duke is caught up in the holocaust simply because he got in the way, and because Andrea had solid reasons to hate him—as Hieronimo did not. The play's catastrophe feeds Andrea's appetite for awful revenge, as indeed Revenge had promised. The presiding deity at the end, in the cosmic world of the play and in the theatre, is Revenge. This is his show. All the engaging metatheatricality of the play-within-the-play, obscuring the demarcation between substance and appearance, role and identity, lends itself to a demonstration of the demonic power of theatre to create an environment in which revenge becomes its own justification and moral questioning of the universe gives way to sensational entertainment.

Kyd's theatrical amorality is all the more stunning in view of his use of a second plot about Villuppo and Alexandro at the court of Portugal. This story, so tangentially connected, can be cut out of performance without leaving a single scar. Its characters play no essential role in the lives of Hieronimo and Bel-imperia, though the fact that the Portuguese Viceroy is Balthazar's father does establish a tenuous link. What this second plot does do, on the other hand, is to offer an illustration of divine justice that seems to work, if only at the last moment. Villippo is the Portuguese counterpart of Lorenzo in that he villainously undertakes to cut down a virtuous adversary for his own mean-spirited advantage. He accuses Alexandro of having assassinated Prince Balthazar on the field of battle in order that Villuppo might supplant Alexandro as the Viceroy's chief adviser. The device works with transparent ease, thereby showing how common it is for kings to be credulous and paranoid; having lost his son, as he thinks, the Viceroy is ready to believe the worst about his most trusted of counsellors without the slightest confirming evidence. The plot very nearly succeeds; Alexandro is already tied to the stake to be burned alive when the Ambassador arrives with news we have long known, that Balthazar is thriving at the Spanish court. Appearances are deceiving, and villainy may flourish for a while, but ultimately heaven will provide deliverance to those who persevere in goodness (III.i). What a different conclusion from that of the main plot! The chorus figures understandably take no notice of Villippo and the hideous death now in store for him. Kyd, as master dramatist with even more authority in the theatre than the impresario Revenge, allows both plots to run their course and to offer contradictory views on the dilemmas of human justice.

When we remember that Proserpina has decreed in the first scene of underworld justice that Balthazar is to die at the hands of Bel-imperia (I.i.89), we understand in retrospect that Fate has decreed this tragedy. Bel-imperia, Hieronimo and the rest are agents of the inevitable, whether they are villains or practitioners of virtue. Kyd's tactic of informing us from the very start of the story's inevitability is part of his dramatic method of dramatic irony. We as audience, and Revenge as presiding deity, know more than anyone onstage, though increasingly Hieronimo as plotter comes to share our knowledge of what is to come. Dramatic irony works its theatrical magic again and again: in the scene of Horatio's courtship of Bel-imperia, when we know that the villains are waiting in the wings to do him in; in Pedringano's bravado in the face of his arrest and trial for murder, counting on the protection of Lorenzo that we and even Lorenzo's page know to be false; in the witnessing of 'Soliman and Perseda', when the King and his brother suppose the deaths to be merely stage deaths but which we as audience know to be 'real'. (This last irony is intensified by our understanding of theatrical convention: the deaths in 'Soliman and Perseda' are of course stage deaths in the same sense that the actor playing Revenge is only assuming a role for the duration of the play, and that Bel-imperia is played by a boy.) *The Spanish Tragedy* is built upon irony, upon the ignorance of the characters that they are being used to fulfil the will of the gods.

Kyd's play was so immensely popular that it was revived often. A fourth edition published in 1602 provides five additions not found in the original octavo of 1592, which was seemingly based on a fairly neat authorial manuscript, though not without its occasional problems that might have resulted from a mix of copy and from adjustments made to the text for public performance. Interim editions in 1594 and 1599 offer nothing of importance other than to attest to the play's continued success. Nor do a number of seventeenth-century editions after 1602. The additions of that year are substantial, but they are unlikely to represent Kyd's own work before he died in 1594. Ben Jonson was paid for some additions to 'Jeronymo' by theatrical manager Philip Henslowe in 1601, in time to be included in the 1602 edition, though the style of the additions we have does not seem convincingly Jonsonian; either he tried to write in a bombast style for a play he had publicly deplored as old-fashioned (in the Induction to *Cynthia's Revels*, 1600) or we must look for some other author-reviser. In any case, some at least of the additions were meant to replace existing scenes, to help rescue the play from seeming out of date and to gratify audiences with more of the sensational stuff that had worked so well in Kyd's beloved warhorse. From 1592, when the first recorded performance took place at the Rose Theatre by Lord Strange's men and Edward Alleyn no doubt in the lead role, the play enjoyed an enviable theatrical run: twenty performances in 1592 (as recorded by Henslowe, Alleyn's partner and stepfather-in-law), a few in 1592–3, and a good number more in 1596–7. Thomas Dekker taunted Ben Jonson with playing Hieronimo in a company of strolling players, perhaps in 1597. The play lived on into the seventeenth century. The twentieth century has seen a handful of revivals, though it is not what one would call a fixture of the stock repertory.

For suggestions on further reading see pp. 145–7 below.

THE
SPANISH TRAGEDY

[DRAMATIS PERSONAE

Ghost of ANDREA.
REVENGE.

KING of Spain ('Spanish King').
CYPRIAN, Duke of Castile ('Castile', 'Duke'), *his brother.*
LORENZO, *the Duke's son.*
BEL-IMPERIA, *Lorenzo's sister.*
GENERAL *of the Spanish Army.*

VICEROY of Portugal ('King').
PEDRO, *his brother.*
BALTHAZAR ('Prince'), *his son.*
ALEXANDRO, ⎱ *noblemen at the Portuguese court.*
VILLUPPO, ⎰
AMBASSADOR *of Portugal to the Spanish court.*

HIERONIMO, *Knight Marshal of Spain.*
ISABELLA, *his wife.*
HORATIO, *his son.*

PEDRINGANO, *servant to Bel-imperia.*
SERBERINE, *servant to Balthazar.*
CHRISTOPHIL, *servant to Lorenzo.*
Page ('Boy') *to Lorenzo.*
Three Watchmen.
Messenger.
Deputy.
Hangman.
Maid *to Isabella.*
Two Portuguese.
Servant.
Three Citizens.
An Old Man, BAZULTO ('Senex').
Portuguese Nobles, Soldiers, Officers, Attendants, Halberdiers.

Three Knights, Three Kings, a Drummer *in the first Dumb-show.*
Hymen, Two Torch-bearers *in the second Dumb-show.*

In HIERONIMO's play:

SOLIMAN, Sultan of Turkey (BALTHAZAR).
ERASTO ('Erastus'), Knight of Rhodes (LORENZO).
Bashaw (HIERONIMO).
PERSEDA (BEL-IMPERIA).

In the Additions:

PEDRO ⎱ *servants to Hieronimo.*
JAQUES ⎰
A Painter, BAZARDO.]

noted for adopting Cynica to English stage → highly rhetorical speeches → stylistic influence

element of madness

The Spanish Tragedy

play about revenge

CONTAINING THE LAMENTABLE END
OF DON HORATIO AND BEL-IMPERIA:
WITH THE PITIFUL DEATH
OF OLD HIERONIMO.

first real English revenge tragedy)

first in English drama

Machiavellian character: Lorenzo. will do anything to help himself out

Act I

[I. i]

corruption in Spain + Portugal

time of Spanish armada (1588)

Enter the Ghost of ANDREA, *and with him* REVENGE.

Andrea. When this eternal substance of my soul
    Did live imprisoned in my wanton flesh,
    Each in their function serving other's need,
    I was a courtier in the Spanish court.
    My name was Don Andrea, my descent,   5
    Though not ignoble, yet inferior far
    To gracious fortunes of my tender youth;
    For there in prime and pride of all my years,
    By duteous service and deserving love,
    In secret I possessed a worthy dame,   10
    Which hight sweet Bel-imperia by name.
    But in the harvest of my summer joys

suggesting they've had sex

too bold, this doesn't happen?

revenge + justice

I.i.] The choric characters of this 'frame' plot are imagined to have come from Hades to the court of Spain (see ll. 86–91), where they will sit and witness the play itself as the unfolding of Andrea's tragedy.

2. *wanton*] rebellious, lascivious.

6–7. *yet . . . youth*] Andrea's rank was not equal to that of the princess whom 'gracious fortune' prompted him to fall in love with.

8. *prime and pride*] the spring-time and most flourishing condition of human life.

11. *Which hight*] who was called.

Death's winter nipped the blossoms of my bliss,
Forcing divorce betwixt my love and me.
For in the late conflict with Portingale   15
My valour drew me into danger's mouth,
Till life to death made passage through my wounds.
When I was slain, my soul descended straight
To pass the flowing stream of Acheron;
But churlish Charon, only boatman there,   20
Said that my rites of burial not performed,
I might not sit amongst his passengers.
Ere Sol had slept three nights in Thetis' lap
And slaked his smoking chariot in her flood,
By Don Horatio, our Knight Marshal's son,   25
My funerals and obsequies were done.
Then was the ferryman of hell content
To pass me over to the slimy strand
That leads to fell Avernus' ugly waves;
There pleasing Cerberus with honeyed speech,   30

---

14. *divorce*] separation.
15. *late*] recent.
Portingale] Portugal.
17.] until my life (i.e. my soul) escaped through my wounds to the land of the dead. The following journey of the soul to the underworld is based upon Virgil's *Aeneid*, Bk VI.
18. *straight*] straightway, at once.
19. *Acheron*] one of the rivers of the lower world.
20. *Charon*] This boatman of the lower world normally ferried the dead across the Styx to Hades.
21.] Without proper burial rites, the souls of the dead were doomed to roam restlessly.
23–4.] i.e. before three nights had passed. At evening, Sol or the sun is imagined going to bed with Thetis, a sea-maiden and daughter of the old man of the sea (Nereus), quenching the daily heat of the sun's chariot in the 'flood' or ocean.
25. *Knight Marshal*] Marshal of the King's House, whose authority in England at that time extended to hearing and determining all pleas of the crown; he handled lawsuits, and judged and awarded punishments for transgressions committed within twelve miles of the court.
28. *strand*] shore.
29. *fell*] cruel, terrible.
Avernus] a lake in the vicinity of Naples, near a cave through which Aeneas descended to the lower world (*Aeneid*, Bk VI).
30. *Cerberus*] a many-headed dog guarding Hades.

I passed the perils of the foremost porch.
Not far from hence, amidst ten thousand souls,
Sat Minos, Aeacus, and Rhadamanth,
To whom no sooner gan I make approach,
To crave a passport for my wand'ring ghost,   35
But Minos, in graven leaves of lottery,
Drew forth the manner of my life and death.
'This knight,' quoth he, 'both lived and died in love,
And for his love tried fortune of the wars,
And by war's fortune lost both love and life.'   40
'Why then,' said Aeacus, 'convey him hence,
To walk with lovers in our fields of love,
And spend the course of everlasting time
Under green myrtle trees and cypress shades.'
'No, no,' said Rhadamanth, 'it were not well   45
With loving souls to place a martialist;
He died in war, and must to martial fields,
Where wounded Hector lives in lasting pain,
And Achilles' Myrmidons do scour the plain.'
Then Minos, mildest censor of the three,   50
Made this device to end the difference.
'Send him,' quoth he, 'to our infernal king,
To doom him as best seems his majesty.'
To this effect my passport straight was drawn.
In keeping on my way to Pluto's court,   55
Through dreadful shades of ever-glooming night,
I saw more sights than thousand tongues can tell,
Or pens can write, or mortal hearts can think.

---

33. *Minos, Aeacus, and Rhadamanth*] appointed judges in the underworld
because of the justice and integrity of their lives. Minos had the casting vote,
as in ll. 50–3.

36–7.] Minos drew forth from an urn the lottery slip on which Andrea's
lot (i.e. the 'manner of his life and death') was engraved.

46. *martialist*] warrior; one born under Mars.

47. *must to*] must go to.

48–9.] In Homer's *Iliad*, Bk XXII, Achilles' Greek Myrmidons or military
followers assist him in slaying the Trojan leader Hector and desecrating his
dead body.

49. *scour*] range swiftly over.

53. *doom*] give judgement on.

55. *Pluto*] ruler of Hades.

Three ways there were: that on the right-hand side
Was ready way unto the foresaid fields,   60
Where lovers live, and bloody martialists,
But either sort contained within his bounds.
The left-hand path, declining fearfully,
Was ready downfall to the deepest hell,
Where bloody Furies shakes their whips of steel,   65
And poor Ixion turns an endless wheel;
Where usurers are choked with melting gold,
And wantons are embraced with ugly snakes,
And murderers groan with never-killing wounds,
And perjured wights scalded in boiling lead,   70
And all foul sins with torments overwhelmed.
'Twixt these two ways, I trod the middle path,
Which brought me to the fair Elysian green,
In midst whereof there stands a stately tower,
The walls of brass, the gates of adamant.   75
Here finding Pluto with his Proserpine,
I showed my passport humbled on my knee,
Whereat fair Proserpine began to smile,
And begged that only she might give my doom.
Pluto was pleased and sealed it with a kiss.   80
Forthwith, Revenge, she rounded thee in th'ear,

---

62. *his*] its.
63.] The left-hand path traditionally leads down to hell; in medieval churches, the stairs leading down to the crypt were on the left-hand side.
64. *downfall*] a sudden descent.
65. *Furies*] primeval avengers of crimes, especially against the ties of kinship.
   shakes] i.e. shake; noun-verb agreements like this are common in Elizabethan English.
66. *Ixion*] His punishment for daring to love Hera or Juno was to be bound to an endlessly turning wheel.
70. *wights*] persons.
73. *Elysian green*] The islands or abodes of the blest in Greek mythology are often placed quite apart from Hades, somewhere in the far West, but Virgil places the Elysian fields in the underworld. Kyd does take some liberties.
75. *adamant*] an alleged rock of diamond-like hardness.
76. *Proserpine*] the Greek Persephone, whom Dis (or Pluto), the ruler of Hades, carried off from earth to be his queen.
79. *doom*] sentence.
81. *rounded*] whispered.

play w/in a play

B. we know wrong / (Andrea will have his revenge)

And bade thee lead me through the gates of horn,
Where dreams have passage in the silent night.
No sooner had she spoke but we were here,
I wot not how, in twinkling of an eye.   85
Revenge. Then know, Andrea, that thou art arrived
Where thou shalt see the author of thy death,
Don Balthazar the prince of Portingale,
Deprived of life by Bel-imperia.
Here sit we down to see the mystery,   God was on   90
And serve for Chorus in this tragedy.   the side of
                                                 the innocent

[I. ii]   *appeal: to single combat when someone
              has killed a family member*

Christianity disapproves of personal revenge

Enter Spanish KING, GENERAL, CASTILE, HIERONIMO.

King. Now say, Lord General, how fares our camp?
General. All well, my sovereign liege, except some few   work out
    That are deceased by fortune of the war.   the truth of Andrea's death
King. But what portends thy cheerful countenance,
    And posting to our presence thus in haste?
    Speak, man, hath fortune given us victory?   5
General. Victory, my liege, and that with little loss.
King. Our Portingals will pay us tribute then?
General. Tribute and wonted homage therewithal.
King. Then blest be heaven, and guider of the heavens,   10
    From whose fair influence such justice flows.
Castile. O *multum dilecte Deo, tibi militat aether,*
    Et conjuratae curvato poplite gentes
    Succumbunt: recti soror est victoria juris.

---

82. *gates of horn*] In the *Aeneid,* VI.893–6, there are twin gates of sleep;
from those of horn true visions emerge, from those of ivory, false visions.

90–1.] Andrea and Revenge are to be present throughout the play as they
sit and watch the tragedy, acting as chorus.

90. *mystery*] events with a secret meaning.

I.ii.] Much of the play is placed at the Spanish court.

1. *camp*] army.

5. *posting*] speeding.

8. *Our Portingals*] the Portuguese warriors we have captured.

12–14.] O man much loved of God, for you the heavens fight, and the
conspiring peoples fall on bended knee; victory is the sister of just right. (An
address deriving from *De Tertio Consulatu Honorii,* 96–8, by the Greek poet
Claudian, who lived and wrote in Rome *c.* 395–404 AD.)

King. Thanks to my loving brother of Castile.   15
    But General, unfold in brief discourse
    Your form of battle and your war's success,
    That, adding all the pleasure of thy news
    Unto the height of former happiness,
    With deeper wage and greater dignity   20
    We may reward thy blissful chivalry.
General. Where Spain and Portingale do jointly knit
    Their frontiers, leaning on each other's bound,
    There met our armies in their proud array,
    Both furnished well, both full of hope and fear,   25
    Both menacing alike with daring shows,
    Both vaunting sundry colours of device,
    Both cheerly sounding trumpets, drums and fifes,
    Both raising dreadful clamours to the sky,
    That valleys, hills, and rivers made rebound,   30
    And heaven itself was frighted with the sound.
    Our battles both were pitched in squadron form,
    Each corner strongly fenced with wings of shot.
    But ere we joined and came to push of pike,
    I brought a squadron of our readiest shot   35
    From out our rearward to begin the fight;
    They brought another wing to encounter us.
    Meanwhile our ordnance played on either side,
    And captains strove to have their valours tried.
    Don Pedro, their chief horsemen's colonel,   40
    Did with his cornet bravely make attempt
    To break the order of our battle ranks.
    But Don Rogero, worthy man of war,

---

20. *deeper wage*] more bountiful reward ('wages').
21. *blissful chivalry*] happy skill in arms.
23. *bound*] boundaries.
27.] both sides proudly displaying various heraldic standards or banners.
30. *That*] so that.
32.] both of our armies were set in a square formation.
33. *fenced ... shot*] fortified with flanking divisions of troops equipped with firearms.
34. *push of pike*] close in-fighting.
38. *played*] fired.
41. *cornet*] company of cavalry, so called from the standard carried at its head.

Marched forth against him with our musketeers,
And stopped the malice of his fell approach.   45
While they maintain hot skirmish to and fro,
Both battles join and fall to handy blows,
Their violent shot resembling th' ocean's rage,
When, roaring loud and with a swelling tide,
It beats upon the rampiers of huge rocks,   50
And gapes to swallow neighbour-bounding lands.
Now while Bellona rageth here and there,
Thick storms of bullets rain like winter's hail,
And shivered lances dark the troubled air.
          Pede pes et cuspide cuspis;   55
      Arma sonant armis, vir petiturque viro.
On every side drop captains to the ground,
And soldiers, some ill-maimed, some slain outright;
Here falls a body scindered from his head,
There legs and arms lie bleeding on the grass,   60
Mingled with weapons and unbowelled steeds,
That scattering overspread the purple plain.
In all this turmoil, three long hours and more,
The victory to neither part inclined,
Till Don Andrea, with his brave lanciers,   65
In their main battle made so great a breach
That, half dismayed, the multitude retired;
But Balthazar, the Portingales' young prince,
Brought rescue and encouraged them to stay.
Here-hence the fight was eagerly renewed,   70
And in that conflict was Andrea slain—
Brave man at arms, but weak to Balthazar.

---

47. *handy*] hand-to-hand.
50. *rampiers*] ramparts.
52. *Bellona*] Roman goddess of war.
54. *dark*] darken.
55-6.] Foot against foot, lance against lance; arms clash on arms and man is assailed by man. (Analogies and possible sources have been found in Statius, Virgil and Curtius.)
59. *scindered*] sundered. (A rare form, perhaps due to association with Latin *scindere*, to cleave; *OED*, sv. *sunder*.)
61. *unbowelled*] disembowelled.
65. *lanciers*] lancers, cavalry soldiers armed with lances.
70. *Here-hence*] as a result of this.
72. *to*] compared with.

[Handwritten marginal annotations:]
goddess of war
Full of sense of victory that he is not comprehending. Only satisfied the tragedy at hand.
ironic bc it will all soon be v undermined
complacent while describing major carnage

Yet while the prince, insulting over him,
Breathed out proud vaunts, sounding to our reproach,
Friendship and hardy valour, joined in one,   75
Pricked forth Horatio, our Knight Marshal's son,
To challenge forth that prince in single fight.
Not long between these twain the fight endured,
But straight the prince was beaten from his horse
And forced to yield him prisoner to his foe.   80
When he was taken, all the rest they fled,
And our carbines pursued them to the death,
Till Phoebus waning to the western deep,
Our trumpeters were charged to sound retreat.
King. Thanks, good Lord General, for these good news,   85
And, for some argument of more to come,
Take this and wear it for thy sovereign's sake.
                              Give him his chain.
But tell me now, hast thou confirmed a peace?
General. No peace, my liege, but peace conditional,
That if with homage tribute be well paid,   90
The fury of your forces will be stayed;
And to this peace their viceroy hath subscribed,
                              Give the KING *a paper.*
And made a solemn vow that during life
His tribute shall be truly paid to Spain.
King. These words, these deeds, become thy person well.   95
But now, Knight Marshal, frolic with thy king,
For 'tis thy son that wins this battle's prize. ✳
Hieronimo. Long may he live to serve my sovereign liege,

---

73. *insulting*] exulting insolently.
74. *sounding to*] tending to.
76. *Pricked*] spurred.
80. *him*] himself.
82. *carbines*] soldiers carrying firearms.
83. *deep*] ocean, where Phoebus Apollo, here the sun-god, goes to his rest
for the night, as at I.i.23–4.
84. *retreat*] the signal to call back the attacking force (not a signal to fall
back under pressure).
86. *argument*] token.
89. *but*] except.
91. *stayed*] restrained.
96. *frolic*] be joyous. Hieronimo is not asked to skylark.

And soon decay unless he serve my liege.

A tucket afar off.

King. Nor thou nor he shall die without reward.   100
What means the warning of this trumpet's sound?
General. This tells me that your grace's men of war,
Such as war's fortune hath reserved from death,
Come marching on towards your royal seat
To show themselves before your majesty,   105
For so I gave in charge at my depart.
Whereby by demonstration shall appear
That all (except three hundred or few more)
Are safe returned and by their foes enriched.

The Army enters, BALTHAZAR *between* LORENZO
and HORATIO, *captive.*

King. A gladsome sight; I long to see them here.   110

They enter and pass by.

Was that the warlike prince of Portingale,
That by our nephew was in triumph led?
General. It was, my liege, the prince of Portingale.
King. But what was he that on the other side
Held him by th' arm as partner of the prize?   115
Hieronimo. That was my son, my gracious sovereign,
Of whom, though from his tender infancy
My loving thoughts did never hope but well,
He never pleased his father's eyes till now,
Nor filled my heart with overcloying joys.   120
King. Go let them march once more about these walls,
That staying them we may confer and talk
With our brave prisoner and his double guard.
Hieronimo, it greatly pleaseth us
That in our victory thou have a share,   125
By virtue of thy worthy son's exploit.

Enter [the Army] again.

Bring hither the young prince of Portingale.
The rest march on; but ere they be dismissed,

99.S.D. tucket] a flourish on a trumpet.
101. *warning*] intimation.
106. *gave in charge*] ordered.

We will bestow on every soldier
Two ducats, and on every leader ten,   130
That they may know our largess welcomes them.
                    Exeunt all [the Army] but BALTHAZAR,
                                LORENZO, HORATIO.
Welcome, Don Balthazar, welcome, nephew,
And thou, Horatio, thou art welcome too.
Young prince, although thy father's hard misdeeds,
In keeping back the tribute that he owes,   135
Deserve but evil measure at our hands,
Yet shalt thou know that Spain is honourable.
Balthazar. The trespass that my father made in peace
Is now controlled by fortune of the wars,
And, cards once dealt, it boots not ask why so.   140
His men are slain, a weakening to his realm,
His colours seized, a blot unto his name,
His son distressed, a corsive to his heart;
These punishments may clear his late offence.
King. Ay, Balthazar, if he observe this truce   145
Our peace will grow the stronger for these wars.
Meanwhile live thou, though not in liberty,
Yet free from bearing any servile yoke,
For in our hearing thy deserts were great,
And in our sight thyself art gracious.   150
Balthazar. And I shall study to deserve this grace.
King. But tell me, for their holding makes me doubt,
To which of these twain art thou prisoner?
Lorenzo. To me, my liege.
Horatio.   To me, my sovereign.
Lorenzo. This hand first took his courser by the reins.   155
Horatio. But first my lance did put him from his horse.

---

130. *ducats*] gold coins.
131. *largess*] liberality, bountifulness.
139. *controlled*] held in check, hence, brought to an end, cancelled out.
140. *boots not ask*] does no good to ask.
142. *colours*] military ensign.
143. *corsive*] corrosive.
144.] i.e. These reversals of fortune are signs of divine anger and punishment for the King of Portugal's recent wrongdoings and arrogance.
152. *their holding*] the way that Lorenzo and Horatio are holding you, one on either side.

Stichomythia

Lorenzo. I seized his weapon and enjoyed it first.
Horatio. But first I forced him lay his weapons down.
King. Let go his arm, upon our privilege.   *Let him go.*
          Say, worthy prince, to whether didst thou yield?   160
Balthazar. To him in courtesy, to this perforce.
          He spake me fair, this other gave me strokes;
          He promised life, this other threatened death;
          He wan my love, this other conquered me;
          And truth to say I yield myself to both.   165
Hieronimo. But that I know your grace for just and wise,
          And might seem partial in this difference,
          Enforced by nature and by law of arms,
          My tongue should plead for young Horatio's right.
          He hunted well that was a lion's death,   170
          Not he that in a garment wore his skin;
          So hares may pull dead lions by the beard.
King. Content thee, Marshal, thou shalt have no wrong,
          And for thy sake thy son shall want no right.
          Will both abide the censure of my doom?   175
Lorenzo. I crave no better than your grace awards.

---

157. *enjoyed*] possessed.
159. *upon our privilege*] in the name of, and guaranteed by, my royal prerogative.
160. *whether*] which of the two.
161.] to Lorenzo in courtesy, to Horatio under threat of force.
162. *He spake me fair*] Lorenzo addressed me courteously.
164. *wan*] won.
166. *But that*] were it not that.
  for] to be.
167. *And . . . partial*] and that I might seem guilty of favouritism.
168.] prompted to side with Horatio through natural affection and through my interpretation of the law of arms (which awards the prisoner to his captor).
170–1.] i.e. The successful hunter is he who kills the lion, not the ass who sports himself in a lion's skin which he has found. Hieronimo gives Horatio credit for having vanquished Balthazar in battle and implies that Lorenzo is merely trying to cash in on that brave deed. (Various fables are referred to here and in l. 172, from Erasmus, Syrus, Martial, and Avian.)
172.] Hieronimo's proverb implies that it is easy to do what Lorenzo did, triumphing over one who is already captured.
174. *want*] lack.
175.] Will both of you accept my judgement?

Handwritten note: tensions that lead together to tragedy

Horatio. Nor I, although I sit beside my right.
King. Then by my judgement thus your strife shall end:
    You both deserve and both shall have reward.
    Nephew, thou took'st his weapon and his horse;   180
    His weapons and his horse are thy reward.
    Horatio, thou didst force him first to yield;
    His ransom therefore is thy valour's fee.
    Appoint the sum as you shall both agree.
    But nephew, thou shalt have the prince in guard,   185
    For thine estate best fitteth such a guest;
    Horatio's house were small for all his train.
    Yet in regard thy substance passeth his,
    And that just guerdon may befall desert,
    To him we yield the armour of the prince.   190
    How likes Don Balthazar of this device?
Balthazar. Right well my liege, if this proviso were,
    That Don Horatio bear us company,
    Whom I admire and love for chivalry.
King. Horatio, leave him not that loves thee so.   195
    Now let us hence to see our soldiers paid,
    And feast our prisoner as our friendly guest.   *Exeunt.*

[I. iii]

Handwritten note: Eustace disagrees → Portugese scenes are seen as disposable

Handwritten note (left margin): King of Portugal

    Enter VICEROY, ALEXANDRO, VILLUPPO[, **Attendants**].

Viceroy. Is our ambassador despatched for Spain?
Alexandro. Two days, my liege, are passed since his depart.
Viceroy. And tribute payment gone along with him?
Alexandro. Ay, my good lord.
Viceroy. Then rest we here awhile in our unrest,   5

Handwritten note: one line convo again

177.] Nor I, even if as a result I must forgo my right.
  184.] Settle on an amount of ransom agreed to by the victor and the vanquished, Horatio and Balthazar. (Later, at II.iii.32–8, the amount becomes a matter of negotiation between Spain and Portugal, with the Portuguese Ambassador as negotiator for his viceroy.)
  186. *estate*] social position.
  187–9.] Horatio's house would be too small for all of Balthazar's retinue. Yet since your wealth, Lorenzo, exceeds Horatio's, and in order that merit may receive its just reward . . .
  190. *him*] Horatio.

  I.iii] The scene is at the court of Portugal.

And feed our sorrows with some inward sighs,
For deepest cares break never into tears.
But wherefore sit I in a regal throne?
This better fits a wretch's endless moan.

Falls to the ground.

Yet this is higher than my fortunes reach,   10
And therefore better than my state deserves.
Ay, ay, this earth, image of melancholy,
Seeks him whom fates adjudge to misery.
Here let me lie, now am I at the lowest.

    Qui jacet in terra non habet unde cadat.   15
    In me consumpsit vires fortuna nocendo,
    Nil superest ut jam possit obesse magis.

Yes, Fortune may bereave me of my crown.
Here, take it now. Let Fortune do her worst;
She will not rob me of this sable weed;   20
O no, she envies none but pleasant things.
Such is the folly of despiteful chance!
Fortune is blind and sees not my deserts;
So is she deaf and hears not my laments;
And could she hear, yet is she wilful mad,   25
And therefore will not pity my distress.
Suppose that she could pity me, what then?
What help can be expected at her hands,
Whose foot is standing on a rolling stone
And mind more mutable than fickle winds?   30
Why wail I then, where's hope of no redress?
O yes, complaining makes my grief seem less.

10.] Yet even this misery cannot indicate fully how bad my circumstances really are.

11. *state*] situation.

12. *image of melancholy*] Melancholy, caused by an excess of black bile, the coldest and most dry of the four 'humours' thought to make up human temperament, corresponds with earth, the coldest and most dry of the four elements of creation (earth, water, air and fire).

15–17.] If one lies on the ground, one can fall no further; in me, Fortune has exhausted her power of hurting; there is nothing left that can harm me more. (A medley, from Alanus de Insulis, Seneca, and Kyd's own invention.)

20. *sable weed*] black mourning garment.

21. *envies*] is hostile towards.

22. *despiteful*] spiteful, malicious.

My late ambition hath distained my faith,
My breach of faith occasioned bloody wars,
Those bloody wars have spent my treasure,   35
And with my treasure my people's blood,
And with their blood, my joy and best beloved,
My best beloved, my sweet and only son.
O wherefore went I not to war myself?
The cause was mine, I might have died for both.   · 40
My years were mellow, his but young and green;
My death were natural, but his was forced.

Alexandro. No doubt, my liege, but still the prince survives.

Viceroy. Survives! Ay, where?

Alexandro. In Spain, a prisoner by mischance of war.   45

Viceroy. Then they have slain him for his father's fault.

Alexandro. That were a breach to common law of arms.

Viceroy. They reck no laws that meditate revenge.

Alexandro. His ransom's worth will stay from foul revenge.

Viceroy. No, if he lived the news would soon be here.   50

Alexandro. Nay, evil news fly faster still than good.

Viceroy. Tell me no more of news, for he is dead.

Villuppo. My sovereign, pardon the author of ill news,
    And I'll bewray the fortune of thy son.

Viceroy. Speak on; I'll guerdon thee whate'er it be.   55
    Mine ear is ready to receive ill news,
    My heart grown hard 'gainst mischief's battery.
    Stand up, I say, and tell thy tale at large.

Villuppo. Then hear that truth which these mine eyes have
        seen.
    When both the armies were in battle joined,   60

33.] My recent ambition (to conquer Spain) sullied my power to produce
convincing authority.
  34. *breach of faith*] violation of sacred treaty obligations.
  40. *for both*] for myself and my son (thus sparing his life).
  43.] There's no doubt, your majesty, but that Balthazar is still alive.
  48. *reck*] reckon, heed.
  49. *stay*] preserve him.
  51. *still*] always.
  54. *bewray*] reveal.
  55. *guerdon*] reward.
  58. *Stand up*] Villuppo has been kneeling, and presumably now rises.
at *large*] in full.

Don Balthazar, amidst the thickest troops,
To win renown did wondrous feats of arms.
Amongst the rest I saw him hand to hand
In single fight with their lord general,
Till Alexandro, that here counterfeits   65
Under the colour of a duteous friend,
Discharged his pistol at the prince's back,
As though he would have slain their general;
But therewithal Don Balthazar fell down,
And when he fell, then we began to fly.   70
But had he lived, the day had sure been ours.
Alexandro. O wicked forgery! O traitorous miscreant!
Viceroy. Hold thou thy peace! But now, Villuppo, say,
 Where then became the carcass of my son?
Villuppo. I saw them drag it to the Spanish tents. 75
Viceroy. Ay, ay, my nightly dreams have told me this.
 Thou false, unkind, unthankful, traitorous beast,
 Wherein had Balthazar offended thee,
 That thou shouldst thus betray him to our foes?
 Was't Spanish gold that bleared so thine eyes 80
 That thou couldst see no part of our deserts?
 Perchance because thou art Terceira's lord
 Thou hadst some hope to wear this diadem,
 If first my son and then myself were slain;
 But thy ambitious thought shall break thy neck. 85
 Ay, this was it that made thee spill his blood,
    Take the crown and put it on again.
 But I'll now wear it till thy blood be spilt.
Alexandro. Vouchsafe, dread sovereign, to hear me speak.
Viceroy. Away with him! His sight is second hell.
 Keep him till we determine of his death.   90
     [Exeunt Attendants with ALEXANDRO.]
 If Balthazar be dead, he shall not live.
 Villuppo, follow us for thy reward. *Exit* VICEROY.

---

72. *forgery*] malicious fabrication.
74. *Where then became*] what then became of.
82. *Terceira*] one of the Azores islands, belonging to Portugal.
91. *he*] Alexandro.

Villuppo. Thus have I with an envious forgèd tale
    Deceived the king, betrayed mine enemy,
    And hope for guerdon of my villainy.   *Exit.* 95

[I. iv]

       Enter HORATIO *and* BEL-IMPERIA.

Bel-imperia. Signior Horatio, this is the place and hour
    Wherein I must entreat thee to relate
    The circumstance of Don Andrea's death,
    Who, living, was my garland's sweetest flower,
    And in his death hath buried my delights.   5
Horatio. For love of him and service to yourself,
    I nill refuse this heavy doleful charge,
    Yet tears and sighs, I fear, will hinder me.
    When both our armies were enjoined in fight,
    Your worthy chevalier amidst the thick'st,   10
    For glorious cause still aiming at the fairest,
    Was at the last by young Don Balthazar
    Encountered hand to hand. Their fight was long,
    Their hearts were great, their clamours menacing,
    Their strength alike, their strokes both dangerous.   15
    But wrathful Nemesis, that wicked power,
    Envying at Andrea's praise and worth,
    Cut short his life to end his praise and worth.
    She, she herself, disguised in armour's mask
    (As Pallas was before proud Pergamus),   20
    Brought in a fresh supply of halberdiers,

---

93. *envious*] malicious.
I.iv.7. *nill*] will not.
9. *enjoined*] joined.
11.] striving always to perform the finest deeds for his glorious cause (of honour in Bel-imperia's eyes).
16. *Nemesis*] a (female) personification of the gods' resentment at, and consequent punishment of, insolence (*hubris*) against themselves.
19–20.] The gods often enter the battle in the *Iliad* and in other epics, disguised in armour. By Pergamus (a town in Macedonia), Kyd must have meant Pergamum, roughly sixty miles south-south-east of Troy and often associated with it. The episode is partly from Virgil's *Aeneid*, II.615–16. Pallas is Pallas Athene, patron goddess of Athens and of Greek cities in general.
21. *halberdiers*] soldiers bearing halberds or long-handled bladed spears.

Which paunched his horse and dinged him to the ground.
Then young Don Balthazar with ruthless rage,
Taking advantage of his foe's distress,
Did finish what his halberdiers begun,　　　　　　　　25
And left not till Andrea's life was done.
Then, though too late, incensed with just remorse,
I with my band set forth against the prince,
And brought him prisoner from his halberdiers.

Bel-imperia. Would thou hadst slain him that so slew my love!　30
But then was Don Andrea's carcass lost?

Horatio. No, that was it for which I chiefly strove,
Nor stepped I back till I recovered him.
I took him up and wound him in mine arms,
And, wielding him unto my private tent,　　　　　　35
There laid him down and dewed him with my tears,
And sighed and sorrowed as became a friend.
But neither friendly sorrow, sighs nor tears,
Could win pale Death from his usurpèd right.
Yet this I did, and less I could not do:　　　　　　40
I saw him honoured with due funeral.
This scarf I plucked from off his lifeless arm,
And wear it in remembrance of my friend.

Bel-imperia. I know the scarf; would he had kept it still!
For had he lived he would have kept it still,　　　　45
And worn it for his Bel-imperia's sake,
For 'twas my favour at his last depart.
But now wear thou it both for him and me,
For after him thou hast deserved it best.
But for thy kindness in his life and death,　　　　50
Be sure, while Bel-imperia's life endures,
She will be Don Horatio's thankful friend.

Horatio. And, madam, Don Horatio will not slack
Humbly to serve fair Bel-imperia.

---

22. *paunched*] stabbed in the belly, disembowelled.
dinged] hurled, struck.
27. *remorse*] regret, pity.
35. *wielding*] i.e. carrying.
39. *his usurpèd right*] the right that he, Death, had usurped.
47. *favour*] love gift worn as a token of devotion to the giver.
53. *slack*] be slow.

But now, if your good liking stand thereto,　　　55
I'll crave your pardon to go seek the prince,
For so the duke your father gave me charge.　　*Exit.*
Bel-imperia. Ay, go, Horatio, leave me here alone,
For solitude best fits my cheerless mood.
Yet what avails to wail Andrea's death,　　　60
From whence Horatio proves my second love?
Had he not loved Andrea as he did,
He could not sit in Bel-imperia's thoughts.
But how can love find harbour in my breast
Till I revenge the death of my beloved?　　　65
Yes, second love shall further my revenge.
I'll love Horatio, my Andrea's friend,
The more to spite the prince that wrought his end.
And where Don Balthazar, that slew my love,
Himself now pleads for favour at my hands,　　　70
He shall in rigour of my just disdain
Reap long repentance for his murd'rous deed.
For what was 't else but murd'rous cowardice,
So many to oppress one valiant knight
Without respect of honour in the fight?　　　75
And here he comes that murdered my delight.

Enter LORENZO *and* BALTHAZAR.

Lorenzo. Sister, what means this melancholy walk?
Bel-imperia. That for a while I wish no company.
Lorenzo. But here the prince is come to visit you.
Bel-imperia. That argues that he lives in liberty.　　　80
Balthazar. No, madam, but in pleasing servitude.
Bel-imperia. Your prison then belike is your conceit.
Balthazar. Ay, by conceit my freedom is enthralled.
Bel-imperia. Then with conceit enlarge yourself again.
Balthazar. What if conceit have laid my heart to gage?　　　85

[margin handwritten: Stichomythia]

---

81. *pleasing servitude*] i.e. the pleasant duty that a 'servant' in love owes to
the lady he serves. But Bel-imperia wilfully misunderstands in her reply; see
next note.
82–5.] Perhaps then your prison is only your fancy, in your imagination.—
Yes, truly, since it is through my fancy (of love) that my freedom is put into
servitude.—In that case you can just 'fancy' yourself right back out (of love)
again.—What if my fancy has offered my heart as a pledge?

Bel-imperia. Pay that you borrowed and recover it.
Balthazar. I die if it return from whence it lies.
Bel-imperia. A heartless man and live? A miracle!
Balthazar. Ay, lady, love can work such miracles.
Lorenzo. Tush, tush, my lord, let go these ambages,   90
    And in plain terms acquaint her with your love.
Bel-imperia. What boots complaint, when there's no remedy?
Balthazar. Yes, to your gracious self must I complain,
    In whose fair answer lies my remedy,
    On whose perfection all my thoughts attend,   95
    On whose aspect mine eyes find beauty's bower,
    In whose translucent breast my heart is lodged.
Bel-imperia. Alas, my lord, these are but words of course,
    And but device to drive me from this place.

        She, in going in, lets fall her glove, which HORATIO,
                coming out, takes up.

Horatio. Madam, your glove.   100
Bel-imperia. Thanks, good Horatio, take it for thy pains.
Balthazar. Signior Horatio stooped in happy time.
Horatio. I reaped more grace than I deserved or hoped.
Lorenzo. My lord, be not dismayed for what is past.
    You know that women oft are humorous.   105
    These clouds will overblow with little wind;
    Let me alone, I'll scatter them myself.
    Meanwhile let us devise to spend the time
    In some delightful sports and revelling.
Horatio. The King, my lords, is coming hither straight,   110
    To feast the Portingal ambassador;
    Things were in readiness before I came.

---

86. *that*] that which.
90. *ambages*] roundabout or indirect modes of speech.
92. *boots*] avails.
96. *aspect*] face.
98. *words of course*] conventional or routine phrases.
99. *but device*] merely a device.
99.2. coming out] coming out onstage.
102. *in happy time*] opportunely.
105. *humorous*] temperamental.
107. *Let me alone*] leave the matter to me.

Balthazar. Then here it fits us to attend the King,
　　To welcome hither our ambassador
　　And learn my father and my country's health.   115

　　Enter the Banquet, Trumpets, the KING *and* AMBASSADOR.

King. See, Lord Ambassador, how Spain entreats
　　Their prisoner Balthazar, thy viceroy's son.
　　We pleasure more in kindness than in wars.
Ambassador. Sad is our king, and Portingale laments,
　　Supposing that Don Balthazar is slain.   120
Balthazar. So am I slain, by beauty's tyranny.
　　You see, my lord, how Balthazar is slain:
　　I frolic with the Duke of Castile's son,
　　Wrapped every hour in pleasures of the court,
　　And graced with favours of his majesty.   125
King. Put off your greetings till our feast be done.
　　Now come and sit with us and taste our cheer.
　　　　　　　　　　　　　　　　　　　　Sit to the banquet.
　　Sit down, young prince, you are our second guest.
　　Brother, sit down, and nephew, take your place.
　　Signior Horatio, wait thou upon our cup,   130
　　For well thou hast deservèd to be honoured.
　　Now, lordings, fall to. Spain is Portugal,
　　And Portugal is Spain; we both are friends,
　　Tribute is paid, and we enjoy our right.

---

113. *fits*] befits.

115. *father*] father's.

115.1. Enter the Banquet] Servants bring on a table or tables, chairs, etc.;
the guests sit at l. 127.1. A *banquet* need not be sumptuous in Elizabethan
usage, but the present occasion for a visiting ambassador requires impressive
ceremonial entertainment.

116. *entreats*] treats.

118. *pleasure*] take pleasure.

121.] Perhaps this line is an aside.

125. *graced*] honoured.

130–1.] Horatio is named cupbearer for the occasion in honourable recognition of his service in the fighting.

134. *Tribute*] i.e. the tribute money Portugal must pay according to the
terms of surrender, not the ransom money for Balthazar and other prisoners
of war. The King later offers to return the tribute money if Balthazar marries
Bel-imperia; see II.iii.19.

But where is old Hieronimo, our marshal?   135
He promised us, in honour of our guest,
To grace our banquet with some pompous jest.

Enter HIERONIMO *with a* Drum, *three* Knights, *each his*
scutcheon. Then he fetches three Kings; *they*
take their crowns and them captive.

Hieronimo, this masque contents mine eye,
Although I sound not well the mystery.
Hieronimo. The first armed knight that hung his scutcheon up   140
          He takes the scutcheon and gives it to the KING.
Was English Robert, Earl of Gloucester,
Who, when King Stephen bore sway in Albion,
Arrived with five and twenty thousand men
In Portingale, and by success of war
Enforced the king, then but a Saracen,   145
To bear the yoke of the English monarchy.
King. My lord of Portingale, by this you see
That which may comfort both your king and you,
And make your late discomfort seem the less.
But say, Hieronimo, what was the next?   150
Hieronimo. The second knight that hung his scutcheon up
                    He doth as he did before.
Was Edmund, Earl of Kent in Albion,

---

137. *grace*] adorn, lend grace to.
pompous jest] stately entertainment, masque.
137.1. Drum] drummer.
137.2. scutcheon] shield with coat of arms.
137.2–3. they . . . captive] i.e. the three (English) Knights capture the
three (Iberian) Kings and take away their crowns.
139.] Although I do not fathom the hidden allegorical significance.
142. *King Stephen*] Stephen, a grandson of William the Conqueror and
nephew of Henry I, maintained his claim to the throne of England (Albion)
from 1135 to 1154 through an anarchic dynastic war with Matilda, Henry I's
daughter. Hieronimo's account (ll. 140–57) of the English successes in
Portugal and Spain embroiders the facts. English forces were at the capture
of Lisbon in 1147, but Robert, Earl of Gloucester does not appear to have
been there.
148–9.] The comfort this masque will afford the Portuguese is to know
that things have been worse in the past and that it is Portugal's fate to be
conquered; see also ll. 158–60.

When English Richard wore the diadem.
He came likewise and razèd Lisbon walls,
And took the King of Portingale in fight,   155
For which, and other suchlike service done,
He after was created Duke of York.
King. This is another special argument
   That Portingale may deign to bear our yoke,
   When it by little England hath been yoked.   160
   But now, Hieronimo, what were the last?
Hieronimo. The third and last, not least in our account,
                                Doing as before.
   Was as the rest a valiant Englishman,
   Brave John of Gaunt, the Duke of Lancaster,
   As by his scutcheon plainly may appear.   165
   He with a puissant army came to Spain,
   And took our King of Castile prisoner.
Ambassador. This is an argument for our viceroy,
   That Spain may not insult for her success,
   Since English warriors likewise conquered Spain,   170
   And made them bow their knees to Albion.
King. Hieronimo, I drink to thee for this device,
   Which hath pleased both the Ambassador and me.
   Pledge me, Hieronimo, if thou love the King.
                   Takes the cup of HORATIO.
   My lord, I fear we sit but over-long,   175
   Unless our dainties were more delicate;
   But welcome are you to the best we have.

---

153. *English Richard*] Richard II, during whose reign (1377–99), one of the
king's uncles, Edmund Langley (later Duke of York), fought in 1381–2 not
on the Spanish side, as Hieronimo states, but on the Portuguese side. The
razing of Lisbon's walls is evidently an invention.
   158. *special argument*] pertinent demonstration.
   164. *John . . . Lancaster*] older brother of Edmund Langley (see previous
note) and uncle to Richard II. Kyd's contemporaries seem to have credited
Gaunt with exploits in Spain that are, once again, fanciful.
   166. *puissant*] powerful.
   169. *insult*] exult insolently; compare I.ii.73.
   174. *Pledge me*] drink in response to the toast I propose.
   174.1. *of*] from.
   176. *Unless*] unless it were that.

Now let us in, that you may be dispatched;
I think our council is already set.   *Exeunt omnes.*

[I. v]

Andrea. Come we for this from depth of underground,
  To see him feast that gave me my death's wound?
  These pleasant sights are sorrow to my soul,
  Nothing but league, and love, and banqueting!
Revenge. Be still, Andrea; ere we go from hence   5
  I'll turn their friendship into fell despite,
  Their love to mortal hate, their day to night,
  Their hope into despair, their peace to war,
  Their joys to pain, their bliss to misery.

---

179. *set*] i.e. in session presumably to determine the terms of the negotiation between Spain and Portugal over the marriage of Bel-imperia and
Balthazar (see II.iii.9–21), with which conditions the Ambassador will be
'dispatched' (l. 178) to return to Portugal.

I.v.] Andrea and Revenge have remained onstage throughout, and will do
so henceforth.
  6. *fell despite*] cruel hatred.

Act II

Enter LORENZO *and* BALTHAZAR.

Lorenzo. My lord, though Bel-imperia seem thus coy,
    Let reason hold you in your wonted joy.
    In time the savage bull sustains the yoke,
    In time all haggard hawks will stoop to lure,
    In time small wedges cleave the hardest oak,   5
    In time the flint is pierced with softest shower,
    And she in time will fall from her disdain,
    And rue the sufferance of your friendly pain.
Balthazar. No, she is wilder, and more hard withal
    Than beast, or bird, or tree, or stony wall.   10
    But wherefore blot I Bel-imperia's name?
    It is my fault, not she, that merits blame.
    My feature is not to content her sight,
    My words are rude and work her no delight.
    The lines I send her are but harsh and ill,   15
    Such as do drop from Pan and Marsyas' quill.
    My presents are not of sufficient cost,
    And, being worthless, all my labour's lost.
    Yet might she love me for my valiancy;

II.i.1. *coy*] unresponsive, disdainful (see l. 7).

2–10.] Modelled on Sonnet 47 in Thomas Watson's *Hecatompathia* (1582).

4.] In time all untamed hawks will come down to their bait or lure (and thus submit to the trainer's authority).

8.] and feel sorry for the pain you have endured so patiently for love of her.

13.] My features and shape are not such as to content her sight.

14. *rude*] unpolished.

16. *Pan and Marsyas*] When Pan, the Greek god of flocks and shepherds, challenged Apollo to a contest in flute-playing, King Midas foolishly declared Pan the winner and was punished with ass's ears. Marsyas, a satyr, was flayed alive for his audacity in challenging Apollo to a similar contest.

quill] reed or feather used in writing or in plucking a stringed instrument.

Ay, but that's slandered by captivity.   20
Yet might she love me to content her sire;
Ay, but her reason masters his desire.
Yet might she love me as her brother's friend;
Ay, but her hopes aim at some other end.
Yet might she love me to uprear her state;   25
Ay, but perhaps she hopes some nobler mate.
Yet might she love me as her beauty's thrall;
Ay, but I fear she cannot love at all.

Lorenzo. My lord, for my sake leave these ecstasies,
And doubt not but we'll find some remedy.   30
Some cause there is that lets you not be loved;
First that must needs be known and then removed.
What if my sister love some other knight?

Balthazar. My summer's day will turn to winter's night.

Lorenzo. I have already found a stratagem   35
To sound the bottom of this doubtful theme.
My lord, for once you shall be ruled by me;
Hinder me not, whate'er you hear or see.
By force or fair means will I cast about
To find the truth of all this question out.   40
Ho, Pedringano!

Pedringano.   Signior!

Lorenzo.   *Vien qui presto.*

Enter PEDRINGANO.

Pedringano. Hath your lordship any service to command me?

Lorenzo. Ay, Pedringano, service of import.
And, not to spend the time in trifling words,
Thus stands the case: it is not long, thou know'st,   45
Since I did shield thee from my father's wrath
For thy conveyance in Andrea's love,

---

20. *slandered*] brought into disrepute.
25. *uprear her state*] raise her social rank.
27. *as . . . thrall*] as one who is made captive by her beauty.
29. *ecstasies*] frenzies—literally, the state of being outside oneself.
36.] to get to the bottom of this uncertain matter, as by sounding with nautical line and lead.
37. *for once*] on this occasion (not implying a unique occasion).
41. *Vien qui presto*] Come here quickly. (Italian.)
47. *conveyance*] clandestine or underhand service.

For which thou wert adjudged to punishment.
I stood betwixt thee and thy punishment;
And since, thou know'st how I have favoured thee.　　50
Now to these favours will I add reward,
Not with fair words, but store of golden coin,
And lands and living joined with dignities,
If thou but satisfy my just demand.
Tell truth and have me for thy lasting friend.　　55
Pedringano. Whate'er it be your lordship shall demand,
My bounden duty bids me tell the truth,
If case it lie in me to tell the truth.
Lorenzo. Then, Pedringano, this is my demand:
Whom loves my sister Bel-imperia?　　60
For she reposeth all her trust in thee.
Speak, man, and gain both friendship and reward.
I mean, whom loves she in Andrea's place?
Pedringano. Alas, my lord, since Don Andrea's death
I have no credit with her as before,　　65
And therefore know not if she love or no.
Lorenzo. Nay, if thou dally then I am thy foe,
　　　　　　　　　　　[*Draw his sword.*]
And fear shall force what friendship cannot win.
Thy death shall bury what thy life conceals;
Thou diest for more esteeming her than me.　　70
Pedringano. O stay, my lord!
Lorenzo. Yet speak the truth and I will guerdon thee,
And shield thee from whatever can ensue,
And will conceal whate'er proceeds from thee;
But if thou dally once again, thou diest.　　75
Pedringano. If Madam Bel-imperia be in love—
Lorenzo. What, villain, ifs and ands?　　　[*Offer to kill him.*]

---

50. *since*] since then.
58. *If case*] supposing. Pedringano promises to tell the truth if he is able,
if he knows the answer; but his speech also suggests someone for whom
telling the truth is contingent on circumstances.
59. *demand*] enquiry.
65. *credit*] being trusted and taken into confidence.
77.S.D. Offer to kill him] Lorenzo gestures as though to kill Pedringano,
threatens to kill him.

Pedringano. O stay my lord, she loves Horatio.

                                BALTHAZAR *starts back.*

Lorenzo. What, Don Horatio, our Knight Marshal's son?

Pedringano. Even him, my lord.   80

Lorenzo. Now say but how know'st thou he is her love,
    And thou shalt find me kind and liberal.
    Stand up, I say, and fearless tell the truth.

Pedringano. She sent him letters which myself perused,
    Full fraught with lines and arguments of love,   85
    Preferring him before Prince Balthazar.

Lorenzo. Swear on this cross that what thou say'st is true,
    And that thou wilt conceal what thou hast told.

Pedringano. I swear to both by Him that made us all.

Lorenzo. In hope thine oath is true, here's thy reward;   90
    But if I prove thee perjured and unjust,
    This very sword whereon thou took'st thine oath
    Shall be the worker of thy tragedy.

Pedringano. What I have said is true, and shall for me
    Be still concealed from Bel-imperia.   95
    Besides, your honour's liberality
    Deserves my duteous service, even till death.

Lorenzo. Let this be all that thou shalt do for me:
    Be watchful when, and where, these lovers meet,
    And give me notice in some secret sort.   100

Pedringano. I will, my lord.

Lorenzo. Then shalt thou find that I am liberal.
    Thou know'st that I can more advance thy state
    Than she; be therefore wise and fail me not.
    Go and attend her, as thy custom is,   105
    Lest absence make her think thou dost amiss.

                              Exit PEDRINGANO.

    Why so: *tam armis quam ingenio*;
    Where words prevail not, violence prevails,
    But gold doth more than either of them both.

---

81. *say but how*] only say how.

83. *Stand up*] Pedringano has been cowering and crouching on his knees.

87. *this cross*] i.e. this sword-hilt.

90. *here's thy reward*] Lorenzo gives Pedringano some of the 'golden coin' he promised at l. 52.

95. *still*] for ever.

100. *sort*] manner.

107. tam armis quam ingenio] as much by force as by guile. (Latin.)

How likes Prince Balthazar this stratagem?   110
Balthazar. Both well and ill. It makes me glad and sad:
   Glad, that I know the hinderer of my love,
   Sad, that I fear she hates me whom I love.
   Glad, that I know on whom to be revenged,
   Sad, that she'll fly me if I take revenge.   115
   Yet must I take revenge or die myself,
   For love resisted grows impatient.
   I think Horatio be my destined plague.
   First in his hand he brandishèd a sword,
   And with that sword he fiercely wagèd war,   120
   And in that war he gave me dangerous wounds,
   And by those wounds he forcèd me to yield,
   And by my yielding I became his slave.
   Now in his mouth he carries pleasing words,
   Which pleasing words do harbour sweet conceits,   125
   Which sweet conceits are limed with sly deceits,
   Which sly deceits smooth Bel-imperia's ears,
   And through her ears dive down into her heart,
   And in her heart set him where I should stand.
   Thus hath he ta'en my body by his force,   130
   And now by sleight would captivate my soul;
   But in his fall I'll tempt the destinies,
   And either lose my life or win my love.
Lorenzo. Let's go, my lord; your staying stays revenge.
   Do you but follow me and gain your love;   135
   Her favour must be won by his remove.   *Exeunt.*

[II. ii]

Enter HORATIO *and* BEL-IMPERIA.

Horatio. Now, madam, since by favour of your love
   Our hidden smoke is turned to open flame,
   And that with looks and words we feed our thoughts

---

  125. *sweet conceits*] pleasant figures of speech.
  126. *limed*] i.e. made into snares, like branches coated with lime to snare
birds.
  127. *smooth*] flatter.
  131. *sleight*] trickery.
  132.] but in going about to cause his fall I'll tempt Fate itself.

  II.ii.3. *that*] since.

(Two chief contents, where more cannot be had),
Thus in the midst of love's fair blandishments,   5
Why show you sign of inward languishments?

PEDRINGANO *showeth all to the* PRINCE *and* LORENZO,
placing them in secret [*above*].

Bel-imperia. My heart, sweet friend, is like a ship at sea:
She wisheth port, where, riding all at ease,
She may repair what stormy times have worn,
And, leaning on the shore, may sing with joy   10
That pleasure follows pain, and bliss annoy.
Possession of thy love is th' only port
Wherein my heart, with fears and hopes long tossed,
Each hour doth wish and long to make resort,
There to repair the joys that it hath lost,   15
And, sitting safe, to sing in Cupid's quire
That sweetest bliss is crown of love's desire.
Balthazar. (*Above*) O sleep, mine eyes! See not my love
    profaned.
Be deaf, my ears! Hear not my discontent.
Die, heart! Another joys what thou deserv'st.   20
Lorenzo. [*Aside*] Watch still, mine eyes, to see this love
    disjoined;
Hear still, mine ears, to hear them both lament;
Live, heart, to joy at fond Horatio's fall!
Bel-imperia. Why stands Horatio speechless all this while?
Horatio. The less I speak, the more I meditate.   25
Bel-imperia. But whereon dost thou chiefly meditate?
Horatio. On dangers past, and pleasures to ensue.
Balthazar. [*Aside*] On pleasures past, and dangers to ensue.
Bel-imperia. What dangers and what pleasures dost thou
    mean?

6.2. above] The 1592 edition gives a stage direction, '*Balthazar* aboue',
after l. 17, indicating that he speaks from that location above the main stage.
    10. *leaning*] resting.
    11. *and bliss annoy*] and bliss follows vexation.
    16. *in Cupid's quire*] as one who belongs to Cupid's choir.
    17. *is*] which is.
    20. *joys*] enjoys.
    23. *fond*] foolish or infatuated.

Horatio. Dangers of war, and pleasures of our love.   30
Lorenzo. [*Aside*] Dangers of death, but pleasures none at all.
Bel-imperia. Let dangers go. Thy war shall be with me,
    But such a war as breaks no bond of peace.
    Speak thou fair words, I'll cross them with fair words;
    Send thou sweet looks, I'll meet them with sweet looks;   35
    Write loving lines, I'll answer loving lines;
    Give me a kiss, I'll countercheck thy kiss.
    Be this our warring peace, or peaceful war.
Horatio. But gracious madam, then appoint the field
    Where trial of this war shall first be made.   40
Balthazar. [*Aside*] Ambitious villain, how his boldness grows!
Bel-imperia. Then be thy father's pleasant bower the field,
    Where first we vowed a mutual amity.
    The court were dangerous, that place is safe.
    Our hour shall be when Vesper gins to rise,   45
    That summons home distressful travellers.
    There none shall hear us but the harmless birds;
    Happily the gentle nightingale
    Shall carol us asleep ere we be ware,
    And, singing with the prickle at her breast,   50
    Tell our delight and mirthful dalliance.
    Till then each hour will seem a year and more.
Horatio. But, honey sweet and honourable love,
    Return we now into your father's sight;
    Dangerous suspicion waits on our delight.   55
Lorenzo. [*Aside*] Ay, danger mixed with jealous despite
    Shall send thy soul into eternal night.   *Exeunt.*

---

    45. *Vesper*] the evening star, Hesperus.
    rise] i.e. appear. Actually, Venus, often seen as the evening star in the
west, is about to set.
    46. *distressful travellers*] labourers ('travailers') exhausted with toil.
    48. *Happily*] haply.
    50.] The nightingale was imagined to lean her breast on a thorn and thus
recall the sharp woes of her life as Philomela, ravaged by her brother-in-law
Tereus and deprived of her tongue.
    56. *jealious*] jealous, envious; so spelled to indicate pronunciation in three
syllables.
    57.S.D. Exeunt] Lorenzo and Balthazar exit above, the lovers below.

[II. iii]

> *Enter* KING of Spain, Portingale AMBASSADOR,
> DON CYPRIAN, &c.

King. Brother of Castile, to the prince's love
    What says your daughter Bel-imperia?
Castile. Although she coy it as becomes her kind,
    And yet dissemble that she loves the prince,
    I doubt not, I, but she will stoop in time.   5
    And were she froward, which she will not be,
    Yet herein shall she follow my advice,
    Which is to love him or forgo my love.
King. Then, Lord Ambassador of Portingale,
    Advise thy king to make this marriage up,   10
    For strengthening of our late-confirmèd league;
    I know no better means to make us friends.
    Her dowry shall be large and liberal:
    Besides that she is daughter and half-heir
    Unto our brother here, Don Cyprian,   15
    And shall enjoy the moiety of his land,
    I'll grace her marriage with an uncle's gift,
    And this it is: in case the match go forward,
    The tribute which you pay shall be released,
    And if by Balthazar she have a son,   20
    He shall enjoy the kingdom after us.
Ambassador. I'll make the motion to my sovereign liege,
    And work it if my counsel may prevail.
King. Do so, my lord, and if he give consent,
    I hope his presence here will honour us   25
    In celebration of the nuptial day;
    And let himself determine of the time.
Ambassador. Will't please your grace command me aught
        beside?

II.iii.3.] Although she affect reserve, as it is her natural disposition as a woman to do.

5. *stoop*] submit; come down submissively to her food, like a hawk being tamed. See II.i.4.

6. *froward*] perverse, refractory.

16. *moiety*] half-share. (The other half presumably goes to Lorenzo.)

19.] The King announced earlier that the tribute money has been paid (I.iv.134); here he offers to give it back, on condition of a marriage.

King. Commend me to the king, and so farewell.
    But where's Prince Balthazar to take his leave?   30
Ambassador. That is performed already, my good lord.
King. Amongst the rest of what you have in charge,
    The prince's ransom must not be forgot.
    That's none of mine, but his that took him prisoner,
    And well his forwardness deserves reward: 35
    It was Horatio, our Knight Marshal's son.
Ambassador. Between us there's a price already pitched,
    And shall be sent with all convenient speed.
King. Then once again farewell, my lord.
Ambassador. Farewell, my lord of Castile and the rest. *Exit.*   40
King. Now brother, you must take some little pains
    To win fair Bel-imperia from her will;
    Young virgins must be rulèd by their friends.
    The prince is amiable and loves her well;
    If she neglect him and forgo his love,   45
    She both will wrong her own estate and ours.
    Therefore, whiles I do entertain the prince
    With greatest pleasure that our court affords,
    Endeavour you to win your daughter's thought;
    If she give back, all this will come to naught. *Exeunt.*   50

[II. iv]

    Enter HORATIO, BEL-IMPERIA, *and* PEDRINGANO.

Horatio. Now that the night begins with sable wings
    To overcloud the brightness of the sun,
    And that in darkness pleasures may be done,
    Come, Bel-imperia, let us to the bower,

---

35. *forwardness*] alacrity, zeal. On the negotation about the ransom, see
I.ii.184 and n.
37. *pitched*] settled, determined. This settlement now must be quickly sent
to Portugal for royal confirmation (l. 38).
38. *with all convenient speed*] as quickly as possible.
42. *will*] wilfulness.
43. *friends*] kinsmen, family.
44. *amiable*] kind, loving, and lovable.
50. *give back*] i.e. turn her back on us.

II.iv.] The scene is set in Hieronimo's bower or arbour; see II.ii.42 and
II.iv.4 and 53.1. It is located in the 'garden'; see II.v.7–8.

And there in safety pass a pleasant hour.   5
Bel-imperia. I follow thee, my love, and will not back,
    Although my fainting heart controls my soul.
Horatio. Why, make you doubt of Pedringano's faith?
Bel-imperia. No, he is as trusty as my second self.
    Go, Pedringano, watch without the gate,   10
    And let us know if any make approach.
Pedringano. [*Aside*] Instead of watching, I'll deserve more
    gold
    By fetching Don Lorenzo to this match.
                          Exit PEDRINGANO.
Horatio. What means my love?
Bel-imperia.   I know not what, myself;
    And yet my heart foretells me some mischance.   15
Horatio. Sweet, say not so; fair fortune is our friend,
    And heavens have shut up day to pleasure us.
    The stars, thou seest, hold back their twinkling shine,
    And Luna hides herself to pleasure us.
Bel-imperia. Thou hast prevailed; I'll conquer my misdoubt,   20
    And in thy love and counsel drown my fear.
    I fear no more; love now is all my thoughts.
    Why sit we not? For pleasure asketh ease.
Horatio. The more thou sit'st within these leafy bowers,
    The more will Flora deck it with her flowers.   25
Bel-imperia. Ay, but if Flora spy Horatio here,
    Her jealous eye will think I sit too near.
Horatio. Hark, madam, how the birds record by night,
    For joy that Bel-imperia sits in sight.
Bel-imperia. No, Cupid counterfeits the nightingale,   30
    To frame sweet music to Horatio's tale.
Horatio. If Cupid sing, then Venus is not far.
    Ay, thou art Venus, or some fairer star.

---

   7. *controls*] overmasters. Bel-imperia's passion gets the better of her appre-
hensive judgement that danger is near.
   9.] No, he is virtually my second self, and as such I trust him.
   10. *without*] outside.
   13. *match*] (*a*) meeting; (*b*) amiable sparring between lovers.
   19. *Luna*] the moon.
   25. *Flora*] goddess of fertility and flowers.
   28. *record*] sing.
   31. *frame*] compose.

Goddess of love   *Goddess of war*

Bel-imperia. If I be Venus thou must needs be Mars,
    And where Mars reigneth there must needs be wars.   35
Horatio. Then thus begin our wars: put forth thy hand,
    That it may combat with my ruder hand.
Bel-imperia. Set forth thy foot to try the push of mine.
Horatio. But first my looks shall combat against thine.
Bel-imperia. Then ward thyself. I dart this kiss at thee.   40
Horatio. Thus I retort the dart thou threw'st at me.
                      [*They kiss.*]
Bel-imperia. Nay then, to gain the glory of the field,
    My twining arms shall yoke and make thee yield.
Horatio. Nay then, my arms are large and strong withal;
    Thus elms by vines are compassed till they fall.   45
Bel-imperia. O, let me go, for in my troubled eyes
    Now may'st thou read that life in passion dies.
Horatio. O, stay awhile and I will die with thee;
    So shalt thou yield and yet have conquered me.
Bel-imperia. Who's there? Pedringano! We are betrayed!   50

   Enter LORENZO, BALTHAZAR, SERBERINE, PEDRINGANO,
                disguised.

Lorenzo. My lord, away with her, take her aside.
    O sir, forbear, your valour is already tried.
    Quickly despatch, my masters.
               They hang him in the arbour.
Horatio. What, will your murder me?
Lorenzo. Ay, thus, and thus! These are the fruits of love.   55
               They stab him.

---

37. *ruder*] rougher, more coarse.
40. *ward*] guard.
42–3.] Bel-imperia suggests that she will pull Horatio down into an amorous coupling.
44. *withal*] in addition.
47–8. *dies . . . die with thee*] with a suggestion of orgasm; a common Elizabethan conceit.
52. *tried*] tested. Lorenzo wryly jests that Horatio has already shown great valour—as a wooer in the 'conquest' of his fair adversary.
53.1.] The woodcut on the title page of the 1615 text of *The Spanish Tragedy* shows a trellis-like arbour, adorned with 'leaves', arched at the top, not wide, but quite deep, and high enough that Horatio can be hanged in it.

Bel-imperia. O, save his life and let me die for him!
  O, save him, brother, save him, Balthazar.
  I loved Horatio, but he loved not me.
Balthazar. But Balthazar loves Bel-imperia.
Lorenzo. Although his life were still ambitious proud,   60
  Yet is he at the highest now he is dead.
Bel-imperia. Murder! Murder! Help, Hieronimo, help!
Lorenzo. Come, stop her mouth. Away with her.
                    Exeunt[, *leaving Horatio's body*].

[II. v]

          Enter HIERONIMO *in his shirt,* &c.

Hieronimo. What outcries pluck me from my naked bed,
  And chill my throbbing heart with trembling fear,
  Which never danger yet could daunt before?
  Who calls Hieronimo? Speak, here I am.
  I did not slumber, therefore 'twas no dream.   5
  No, no, it was some woman cried for help,
  And here within this garden did she cry,
  And in this garden must I rescue her.
  But stay, what murd'rous spectacle is this?
  A man hanged up and all the murderers gone,   10
  And in my bower, to lay the guilt on me?
  This place was made for pleasure not for death.
                    He cuts him down.
  Those garments that he wears I oft have seen—
  Alas, it is Horatio, my sweet son!
  O no, but he that whilom was my son.   15
  O, was it thou that call'dst me from my bed?
  O speak, if any spark of life remain.
  I am thy father. Who hath slain my son?

60–1.] Lorenzo makes a grisly joke: Horatio's presumption in aspiring to the love of Bel-imperia has led to his 'elevation' in a noose.

II.v.] The scene continues; the marking of a new scene is editorial convention.
0.1. shirt] nightshirt.
1. *naked bed*] This common phrase originated in the custom of sleeping naked.
15. *whilom*] formerly, in the past.

What savage monster, not of human kind,
Hath here been glutted with thy harmless blood,   20
And left thy bloody corpse dishonoured here,
For me amidst this dark and deathful shades
To drown thee with an ocean of my tears?
O heavens, why made you night to cover sin?
By day, this deed of darkness had not been.   25
O earth, why didst thou not in time devour
The vile profaner of this sacred bower?
O poor Horatio, what hadst thou misdone,
To leese thy life ere life was new begun?
O wicked butcher, whatsoe'er thou wert,   30
How could thou strangle virtue and desert?
Ay me most wretched, that have lost my joy,
In leesing my Horatio, my sweet boy!

Enter ISABELLA.

Isabella. My husband's absence makes my heart to throb—
    Hieronimo!   35
Hieronimo. Here Isabella, help me to lament,
    For sighs are stopped, and all my tears are spent.
Isabella. What world of grief—My son Horatio!
    O, where's the author of this endless woe?
Hieronimo. To know the author were some ease of grief,   40
    For in revenge my heart would find relief.
Isabella. Then is he gone? And is my son gone too?
    O gush out, tears, fountains and floods of tears,
    Blow, sighs, and raise an everlasting storm!
    For outrage fits our cursèd wretchedness.   45
                              [*First Addition; see pp. 131–2*]
Hieronimo. Sweet lovely rose, ill-plucked before thy time,

---

22. *this*] these.
29. *leese*] lose.
ere . . . begun] i.e. in one so young, whose life promised so much that now cannot be fulfilled.
31. *desert*] deserving, worth.
38. *What world of grief*] Isabella starts to ask her husband the cause of his sorrow, but breaks off as she sees her son's corpse.
40. *were*] would be.
45. *outrage*] passionate behaviour.

Fair worthy son, not conquered but betrayed,
I'll kiss thee now, for words with tears are stayed.
Isabella. And I'll close up the glasses of his sight,
　For once these eyes were only my delight.　　　　　50
Hieronimo. Seest thou this handkercher besmeared with
　　blood?
　It shall not from me till I take revenge.
　Seest thou those wounds that yet are bleeding fresh?
　I'll not entomb them till I have revenged.
　Then will I joy amidst my discontent;　　　　　55
　Till then my sorrow never shall be spent.
Isabella. The heavens are just; murder cannot be hid;
　Time is the author both of truth and right,
　And time will bring this treachery to light.
Hieronimo. Meanwhile, good Isabella, cease thy plaints,　60
　Or at the least dissemble them awhile;
　So shall we sooner find the practice out,
　And learn by whom all this was brought about.
　Come Isabel, now let us take him up,
　　　　　　　　　　　　　They take him up.
　And bear him in from out this cursèd place.　　　65
　I'll say his dirge; singing fits not this case.
　O aliquis mihi quas pulchrum ver educat herbas
　　　　　　　　HIERONIMO *sets his breast unto his sword.*
　Misceat, et nostro detur medicina dolori;
　Aut, si qui faciunt animis oblivia, succos
　Praebeat. Ipse metam magnum quaecunque per orbem　70
　Gramina Sol pulchras effert in luminis oras.
　Ipse bibam quicquid meditatur saga veneni,
　Quicquid et herbarum vi caeca nenia nectit.
　Omnia perpetiar, lethum quoque, dum semel omnis

---

60. *plaints*] lamentations.
62. *practice*] contrivance, evil scheming.
67–80.] Let someone mix for me herbs which the beautiful spring brings
forth, and let a medicine be given for our pain; or let him offer juices if there
are any which will bring oblivion to our minds. I shall myself gather whatever
herbs the sun brings forth, throughout the mighty world, into the fair realms
of light. I shall myself drink whatever poison the sorceress contrives, whatever herbs, too, the goddess of spells weaves together by her secret power. All

Noster in extincto moriatur pectore sensus. 75
Ergo tuos oculos nunquam, mea vita, videbo,
Et tua perpetuus sepelivit lumina somnus?
Emoriar tecum, sic, sic juvat ire sub umbras.
At tamen absistam properato cedere letho,
Ne mortem vindicta tuam tum nulla sequatur. 80
    Here he throws it from him and bears the body away.

[II. vi]

Andrea. Brought'st thou me hither to increase my pain?
    I looked that Balthazar should have been slain,
    But 'tis my friend Horatio that is slain,
    And they abuse fair Bel-imperia,
    On whom I doted more than all the world, 5
    Because she loved me more than all the world.
Revenge. Thou talk'st of harvest when the corn is green.
    The end is crown of every work well done;
    The sickle comes not till the corn be ripe.
    Be still, and ere I lead thee from this place 10
    I'll show thee Balthazar in heavy case.

---

things I shall essay, death even, until all feeling dies at once in my dead heart. Shall I never again, my life, see your face, and has eternal sleep buried your light? I shall die with you; so, so would I rejoice to go to the shades below. But none the less I shall keep myself from a hasty death, in case then no revenge should follow your death. (A medley of phrases from classical poetry and from Kyd's own invention, as at I.ii.55–6 and I.iii.15–17. Whether or not Kyd's audience could have followed this Latin in the theatre—and quite likely not all of them could, since this was a public theatre—they would have savoured the atmosphere of a kind of dirge, pagan in spirit but akin in a way to a church service for the dead.)

    80.1. it] his sword; see l. 67.1. Hieronimo ends his dirge by disavowing suicide. The action in 64 ff. is not entirely clear. Perhaps Hieronimo and Isabella tend to and half-raise Horatio's corpse at l. 64; Isabella continues to minister to her dead son's body while Hieronimo recites the dirge, sword pointed at his breast; and at the end, having thrown away his sword, Hieronimo carries off the body with or without the aid of Isabella.

    II.vi.2. *looked*] expected.
    11. *in heavy case*] in grave trouble.

Act III

[III. i]

Enter VICEROY of Portingale, Nobles, VILLUPPO.

Viceroy. Infortunate condition of kings,
  Seated amidst so many helpless doubts!
  First we are placed upon extremest height,
  And oft supplanted with exceeding heat,
  But ever subject to the wheel of chance;   5
  And at our highest never joy we so,
  As we both doubt and dread our overthrow.
  So striveth not the waves with sundry winds
  As fortune toileth in the affairs of kings,
  That would be feared, yet fear to be beloved,   10
  Sith fear or love to kings is flattery.
  For instance, lordings, look upon your king,
  By hate deprivèd of his dearest son,
  The only hope of our successive line.
First Noble. I had not thought that Alexandro's heart   15
  Had been envenomed with such extreme hate;
  But now I see that words have several works,

III.i.] The scene is the court of Portugal.

1–11.] An adaptation of Seneca's *Agamemnon*, 57–73.

4. *heat*] passion, anger, fury.

5. *the wheel of chance*] Fortune's wheel, on which the great especially are lifted up and then cast down.

7. *doubt*] fear, suspect.

8–9.] Even the striving of the waves with various winds cannot compare with Fortune's toiling in the affairs of kings.

10. *That would be feared*] who wish to be feared (since awe commands respect and obedience).

11. *Sith*] since.

13. *By hate*] by the alleged malice of Alexandro (see I.iii.65–70); but with further resonances of the enmity between Spain and Portugal, the Viceroy's own sinful ambitions, and the hostility of Fortune.

17. *words have several works*] i.e. words are not always related to deeds.

And there's no credit in the countenance.

Villuppo. No; for, my lord, had you beheld the train
    That feignèd love had coloured in his looks,   20
    When he in camp consorted Balthazar,
    Far more inconstant had you thought the sun,
    That hourly coasts the centre of the earth,
    Than Alexandro's purpose to the prince.

Viceroy. No more, Villuppo, thou hast said enough,   25
    And with thy words thou slay'st our wounded thoughts.
    Nor shall I longer dally with the world,
    Procrastinating Alexandro's death.
    Go some of you and fetch the traitor forth,
    That as he is condemnèd he may die.   30

    Enter ALEXANDRO *with a* Nobleman *and* Halberts.

Second Noble. In such extremes will naught but patience
    serve.
Alexandro. But in extremes what patience shall I use?
    Nor discontents it me to leave the world,
    With whom there nothing can prevail but wrong.
Second Noble. Yet hope the best.
Alexandro.   'Tis Heaven is my hope.   35
    As for the earth, it is too much infect

18.] One cannot know a person by facial expression.

19–20. *had you . . . looks*] i.e. if you had beheld the feigned love in his looks, disguising the treachery of his heart. *Train* means 'treachery'; *coloured* means 'disguised'.

21. *consorted*] kept company with.

23.] that makes its daily round from hour to hour about this centre of the universe, the earth.

27. *dally with the world*] delay the affairs of this world.

30.1. Halberts] Halberdiers; see I.iv.21 and n.

32.] As a virtuous Christian, Alexandro responds to the suggestion that he be patient by suggesting that calm and self-possessed waiting for better fortune can avail him nothing; he will practise instead the patience of worldly renunciation.

34. *With whom*] in which world.

35.] Alexandro's hope in Heaven bespeaks the same Christian resolution he showed in l. 32 above (see note): one must learn to hope not for better fortune but for eternal life.

To yield me hope of any of her mould.
Viceroy. Why linger ye? Bring forth that daring fiend
  And let him die for his accursèd deed.
Alexandro. Not that I fear the extremity of death,   40
  For nobles cannot stoop to servile fear,
  Do I, O king, thus discontented live.
  But this, O this, torments my labouring soul,
  That thus I die suspected of a sin
  Whereof, as heavens have known my secret thoughts,   45
  So am I free from this suggestion.
Viceroy. No more, I say! To the tortures! When!
  Bind him, and burn his body in those flames
                    They bind him to the stake.
  That shall prefigure those unquenchèd fires
  Of Phlegethon preparèd for his soul.   50
Alexandro. My guiltless death will be avenged on thee,
  On thee, Villuppo, that hath maliced thus,
  Or for thy meed hast falsely me accused.
Villuppo. Nay, Alexandro, if thou menace me,
  I'll lend a hand to send thee to the lake   55
  Where those thy words shall perish with thy works,
  Injurious traitor, monstrous homicide!

                    Enter AMBASSADOR.

Ambassador. Stay, hold a while,
  And here, with pardon of his majesty,
  Lay hands upon Villuppo.
Viceroy.   Ambassador,   60

37.] to give me reason to hope for good things from anyone composed of her (the earth's) material. *Mould* means clods of earth, as in a grave; the dust to which all life returns; suggesting also hollow matrix.

46. *suggestion*] false accusation.

47. *When!*] a common exclamation denoting impatience: 'Get on with it!'

48.1. the stake] perhaps a pillar supporting the theatre's roof, or possibly the makings of a funeral pyre are brought onstage for this scene.

50. *Phlegethon*] the fiery river among the four rivers of Hades, here signifying the fires of hell prepared for the damned.

51. *avenged*] i.e. avenged by God's justice.

52. *maliced*] practised malice.

53. *for thy meed*] in hope of reward.

55. *the lake*] Acheron, the infernal lake (or river).

59. *with ... majesty*] with the Viceroy's permission.

What news hath urged this sudden entrance?
Ambassador. Know, sovereign lord, that Balthazar doth live.
Viceroy. What say'st thou? Liveth Balthazar our son?
Ambassador. Your highness' son, Lord Balthazar, doth live,
    And, well entreated in the court of Spain,   65
    Humbly commends him to your majesty.
    These eyes beheld, and these my followers,
    With these, the letters of the King's commends,
                        Gives him letters.
    Are happy witnesses of his highness' health.
              The KING *looks on the letters, and proceeds.*
Viceroy. 'Thy son doth live, your tribute is received,   70
    Thy peace is made, and we are satisfied.
    The rest resolve upon as things proposed
    For both our honours and thy benefit.'
Ambassador. These are his highness' farther articles.
                    He gives him more letters.
Viceroy. [*To Villuppo*] Accursèd wretch, to intimate these ills 75
    Against the life and reputation
    Of noble Alexandro!—Come, my lord,
    Let him unbind thee that is bound to death
    To make a quital for thy discontent.   *They unbind him.*
Alexandro. Dread lord, in kindness you could do no less,   80
    Upon report of such a damnèd fact;
    But thus we see our innocence hath saved
    The hopeless life which thou, Villuppo, sought
    By thy suggestions to have massacred.
Viceroy. Say, false Villuppo, wherefore didst thou thus   85
    Falsely betray Lord Alexandro's life?

---

65. *entreated*] treated.
66. *commends him*] commends himself, sends his greetings.
68. *commends*] greetings, compliments.
72. *The rest resolve upon*] examine and decide about the other matters (contained in the 'farther articles', l. 74).
78–9.] i.e. Let Villuppo, whom I now declare bound to death, unbind you, Alexandro, making *quital* or requital for what you have suffered.
79.S.D. They unbind him] Perhaps those in attendance assist as Villuppo unbinds Alexandro as he has been ordered; or the Viceroy means simply that Villuppo's being taken into custody has the effect of freeing Alexandro.
80. *in kindness*] prompted by natural feeling.
81. *fact*] deed.

Him whom thou know'st that no unkindness else,
But even the slaughter of our dearest son,
Could once have moved us to have misconceived?
Alexandro. Say, treacherous Villuppo, tell the king,   90
    Or wherein hath Alexandro used thee ill?
Villuppo. Rent with remembrance of so foul a deed,
    My guilty soul submits me to thy doom;
    For, not for Alexandro's injuries,
    But for reward, and hope to be preferred,   95
    Thus have I shamelessly hazarded his life.
Viceroy. Which, villain, shall be ransomed with thy death,
    And not so mean a torment as we here
    Devised for him, who thou said'st slew our son,
    But with the bitterest torments and extremes   100
    That may be yet invented for thine end.

                    ALEXANDRO *seems to entreat.*
Entreat me not. Go take the traitor hence.

                    Exit VILLUPPO [*guarded*].
And, Alexandro, let us honour thee
With public notice of thy loyalty.
To end those things articulated here   105
By our great lord, the mighty King of Spain,
We with our council will deliberate.
Come, Alexandro, keep us company.   *Exeunt.*

[III. ii]

Enter HIERONIMO.

Hieronimo. O eyes, no eyes, but fountains fraught with tears!
    O life, no life, but lively form of death!
    O world, no world, but mass of public wrongs,
    Confused and filled with murder and misdeeds!

87–9.] Him whom you know that no accusation short of assassinating my son, the crown prince, could have prompted me to have suspected.
95. *preferred*] promoted, favoured.
97. *ransomed*] atoned for.
98. *mean*] moderate.
105. *articulated*] set forth in the articles of the proposed treaty.

III.ii.] Hieronimo is near the Duke of Castile's house; see ll. 50–2.
2. *lively*] lifelike.

O sacred heavens, if this unhallowed deed,   5
If this inhuman and barbarous attempt,
If this incomparable murder thus
Of mine, but now no more, my son
Shall unrevealed and unrevengèd pass,
How should we term your dealings to be just,   10
If you unjustly deal with those that in your justice trust?
The night, sad secretary to my moans,
With direful visions wake my vexèd soul,
And with the wounds of my distressful son
Solicit me for notice of his death.   15
The ugly fiends do sally forth of hell,
And frame my steps to unfrequented paths,
And fear my heart with fierce inflamèd thoughts.
The cloudy day my discontents records,
Early begins to register my dreams   20
And drive me forth to seek the murderer.
Eyes, life, world, heavens, hell, night, and day,
See, search, show, send, some man, some mean, that
    may—   *A letter falleth.*
What's here? A letter? Tush, it is not so!
A letter written to Hieronimo!   *Red ink.*   25
'For want of ink, receive this bloody writ.
Me hath my hapless brother hid from thee;
Revenge thyself on Balthazar and him,
For these were they that murdered thy son.
Hieronimo, revenge Horatio's death,   30
And better fare than Bel-imperia doth.'
What means this unexpected miracle?
My son slain by Lorenzo and the prince!

---

12. *sad . . . moans*] the confidant to whom my moans are uttered.
13, 15. *wake . . . Solicit*] wakes . . . Solicits.
15.] (The night) urges me to make clamour over Horatio's death.
17. *frame*] direct.
18. *fear*] frighten.
21. *drive*] drives.
23. *mean*] means.
25.S.D. Red ink] Probably this is Kyd's note to the acting company (or, possibly, the prompter's reminder) that red ink is to be used for the letter, since it is supposedly written in Bel-imperia's blood.
27. *hapless*] ill-starred.

What cause had they Horatio to malign?
Or what might move thee, Bel-imperia,   35
To accuse thy brother, had he been the mean?
Hieronimo, beware, thou art betrayed,
And to entrap thy life this train is laid.
Advise thee therefore, be not credulous;
This is devisèd to endanger thee,   40
That thou by this Lorenzo shouldst accuse,
And he, for thy dishonour done, should draw
Thy life in question and thy name in hate.
Dear was the life of my belovèd son,
And of his death behoves me be revenged;   45
Then hazard not thine own, Hieronimo,
But live t' effect thy resolution.
I therefore will by circumstances try
What I can gather to confirm this writ,
And, heark'ning near the Duke of Castile's house,   50
Close if I can with Bel-imperia,
To listen more, but nothing to bewray.

Enter PEDRINGANO.

Now, Pedringano!
Pedringano.   Now, Hieronimo!
Hieronimo. Where's thy lady?
Pedringano.   I know not; here's my lord.

Enter LORENZO.

Lorenzo. How now, who's this? Hieronimo?
Hieronimo.   My lord.   55
Pedringano. He asketh for my lady Bel-imperia.
Lorenzo. What to do, Hieronimo? The duke my father hath
     Upon some disgrace awhile removed her hence,
     But if it be aught I may inform her of,

---

38. *train*] snare, trap.
48. *circumstances*] circumstantial evidence, other information.
51. *Close*] conjoin, come into close contact.
52. *bewray*] reveal.
52.1, 54.1.] Pedringano and then Lorenzo enter as though from the Duke
of Castile's house. Lorenzo is suspicious of Hieronimo's being there,
uninvited.

Tell me, Hieronimo, and I'll let her know it.   60
Hieronimo. Nay, nay, my lord, I thank you, it shall not need;
    I had a suit unto her, but too late,
    And her disgrace makes me unfortunate.
Lorenzo. Why so, Hieronimo? Use me.
Hieronimo. O no, my lord, I dare not, it must not be.   65
                    [*Second Addition; see p. 133*]
    I humbly thank your lordship.
Lorenzo.   Why then, farewell.
Hieronimo. [*Aside*] My grief no heart, my thoughts no
    tongue can tell.   *Exit.*
Lorenzo. Come hither, Pedringano, seest thou this?
Pedringano. My lord, I see it, and suspect it too.
Lorenzo. This is that damnèd villain Serberine,   70
    That hath, I fear, revealed Horatio's death.
Pedringano. My lord, he could not, 'twas so lately done,
    And since, he hath not left my company.
Lorenzo. Admit he have not, his condition's such,
    As fear or flattering words may make him false.   75
    I know his humour, and therewith repent
    That e'er I used him in this enterprise.
    But Pedringano, to prevent the worst,
    And 'cause I know thee secret as my soul,
    Here for thy further satisfaction take thou this,   80
                    Gives him more gold.
    And hearken to me—thus it is devised:
    This night thou must, and prithee so resolve,
    Meet Serberine at Saint Luigi's Park—
    Thou know'st 'tis here hard by behind the house;
    There take thy stand, and see thou strike him sure,   85
    For die he must, if we do mean to live.

---

61. *it shall not need*] there's no need.
64. *Use me*] put your suit to me.
68. *this*] i.e. Hieronimo's snooping around.
70. *Serberine*] Balthazar's servant, who enters disguised with his master at
II.iv.50.1 to murder Horatio, and whom Lorenzo here suspects of having
talked.
73. *since*] since that time.
74.] Even if he hasn't been out of your sight, his nature is such.
76. *humour*] disposition.

Pedringano. But how shall Serberine be there, my lord?
Lorenzo. Let me alone, I'll send to him to meet
    The prince and me, where thou must do this deed.
Pedringano. It shall be done, my lord, it shall be done,   90
    And I'll go arm myself to meet him there.
Lorenzo. When things shall alter, as I hope they will,
    Then shalt thou mount for this. Thou know'st my
       mind.   *Exit* PEDRINGANO.
    Che le Ieron!

you'll be Promoted [handwritten annotation]

Enter Page.

Page.   My lord?
Lorenzo.   Go, sirrah, to Serberine,
    And bid him forthwith meet the prince and me   95
    At Saint Luigi's Park, behind the house—
    This evening, boy!
Page.   I go, my lord.
Lorenzo. But sirrah, let the hour be eight o'clock.
    Bid him not fail.
Page.   I fly, my lord.   *Exit.*
Lorenzo. Now to confirm the complot thou hast cast   100
    Of all these practices, I'll spread the watch,
    Upon precise commandment from the King,
    Strongly to guard the place where Pedringano
    This night shall murder hapless Serberine.
    Thus must we work that will avoid distrust;   105
    Thus must we practise to prevent mishap,

---

88. *Let me alone*] leave it to me. (As at I.iv.107.)

93. *mount*] (*a*) be promoted; (*b*) mount the scaffold to be hanged. Pedringano presumably does not grasp the second meaning, which is Lorenzo's little joke for the audience's benefit. Compare his similarly grisly humour at II.iv.60–1 and n.

94. *Che le Ieron*] apparently a corruption of a summons or other form of address to the Page, possibly *Que, ladrón!* (French: *larron*), 'What, you little thief!'

sirrah] a form of address to inferiors.

100–2.] Now, to bring to fulfilment the plot that you, Lorenzo, have contrived by all this cunning deception, I'll station the night watch, making it seem as though the order comes explicitly from the King. (Lorenzo gloats to himself.)

105.] Thus must I undertake that which will avert suspicion.

And thus one ill another must expulse.
This sly enquiry of Hieronimo
For Bel-imperia breeds suspicion,
And this suspicion bodes a further ill.   110
As for myself, I know my secret fault,
And so do they, but I have dealt for them.
They that for coin their souls endangerèd,
To save my life, for coin shall venture theirs;
And better it's that base companions die   115
Than by their life to hazard our good haps.
Nor shall they live for me to fear their faith.
I'll trust myself; myself shall be my friend;
For die they shall. Slaves are ordained to no other end.
                                                    Exit.

[III. iii]

Enter PEDRINGANO *with a pistol.*

Pedringano. Now, Pedringano, bid thy pistol hold,
      And hold on, Fortune! Once more favour me,
      Give but success to mine attempting spirit,
      And let me shift for taking of mine aim!
      Here is the gold, this is the gold proposed;   5
      It is no dream that I adventure for,
      But Pedringano is possessed thereof.
      And he that would not strain his conscience
      For him that thus his liberal purse hath stretched,

---

111. *fault*] misdeed, offence.
112. *they*] Pedringano and Serberine, whose fates are sealed.
113–14.] To save my own skin and further my fortunes, I will risk the lives of those who, for their private gain, have endangered their souls (by committing murder).
115.] it's better that low-bred fellows die.
117. *fear their faith*] worry about their keeping faith.

III.iii.] The scene takes place at St Luigi's park.
1. *hold*] hold fast, be true.
2. *hold on*] hold steady.
4.] And I'll look after pointing the pistol.
5–7.] i.e. the gold that is to be my reward is no dream; it's right here in my hand.

Unworthy such a favour may he fail,   10
And, wishing, want, when such as I prevail.
As for the fear of apprehension,
I know, if need should be, my noble lord
Will stand between me and ensuing harms.
Besides, this place is free from all suspect.   15
Here therefore will I stay and take my stand.

Enter the Watch.

First Watch. I wonder much to what intent it is
   That we are thus expressly charged to watch.
Second Watch. 'Tis by commandment in the King's own
   name.
Third Watch. But we were never wont to watch and ward   20
   So near the duke his brother's house before.
Second Watch. Content yourself, stand close; there's
   somewhat in't.

Enter SERBERINE.

Serberine. Here, Serberine, attend and stay thy pace,
   For here did Don Lorenzo's page appoint
   That thou by his command shouldst meet with him.   25
   How fit a place, if one were so disposed,
   Methinks this corner is to close with one!
Pedringano. [*Aside*] Here comes the bird that I must seize
   upon.

10–11.] May such a fellow fail as unworthy of the favour offered him, and
continue to suffer privation in mockery of his desires, while enterprising
fellows like me prosper.

15. *suspect*] suspicion.

20. *watch and ward*] patrol, keep a guard. Originally part of the legal
definition of the duties of a sentinel.

21. *the . . . house*] the house of the Duke of Castile, the King's brother.

22.] Don't fret about it, stand concealed; there's something going on.

23.] Serberine is nervously talking to himself. In the dark, Pedringano
and the Watch are as yet unaware of the other's presence, and Serberine
enters thinking he is alone. (This darkness is a matter of stage convention;
the audience can see everyone, especially in an Elizabethan public theatre
with performance very likely in the afternoon and the theatre open to the
sky.)

27. *close with one*] attack somebody at close quarters.

Now, Pedringano, or never play the man!
Serberine. I wonder that his lordship stays so long,   30
Or wherefore should he send for me so late?
Pedringano. For this, Serberine, and thou shalt ha't.
                        Shoots the dag. [Serberine falls.]
So, there he lies; my promise is performed.

                The Watch [*step forward*].

First Watch. Hark, gentlemen, this is a pistol shot.
Second Watch. And here's one slain. Stay the murderer.   35
Pedringano. Now by the sorrows of the souls in hell,
                        He strives with the Watch.
Who first lays hand on me, I'll be his priest.
Third Watch. Sirrah, confess, and therein play the priest,
Why hast thou thus unkindly killed the man?
Pedringano. Why? Because he walked abroad so late.   40
Third Watch. Come, sir, you had been better kept your bed
Than have committed this misdeed so late.
Second Watch. Come, to the Marshal's with the murderer!
First Watch. On to Hieronimo's! Help me here
To bring the murdered body with us too.   45
Pedringano. Hieronimo! Carry me before whom you will.
Whate'er he be, I'll answer him and you,

29.] Pedringano pumps himself up to perform the murder by telling himself that it's now or never if he is to prove his manhood.

31. *wherefore*] why.

32. *For this*] Pedringano jests grimly: here is what Lorenzo bade you come here for.

32.1. *dag*] a kind of heavy pistol or handgun.

33.1.] The phrase in the original text, '*The* Watch', is not an entrance stage direction but seems instead to indicate that the members of the Watch we have to step forward and confront Pedringano with his shooting of Serberine.

37. *I'll be his priest*] i.e. I'll smooth his passage to the next world, make an end of him.

38. *confess*] The Third Watch answers Pedringano with a gibe: 'If you want to play the priest, then make your confession.' (Strictly speaking, a priest confesses by hearing the confession of a penitent, not by confessing in the Third Watch's sense.)

39. *unkindly*] unnaturally; ungenerously.

40. *abroad*] out of doors; from home.

42. *so late*] (*a*) just now; (*b*) so late at night (as in l. 40).

And do your worst, for I defy you all.

Exeunt [with Serberine's body].

[III. iv]

Enter LORENZO *and* BALTHAZAR.

Balthazar. How now, my lord, what makes you rise so soon?
Lorenzo. Fear of preventing our mishaps too late.
Balthazar. What mischief is it that we not mistrust?
Lorenzo. Our greatest ills we least mistrust, my lord,
And inexpected harms do hurt us most.   5
Balthazar. Why, tell me, Don Lorenzo, tell me, man,
If aught concerns our honour and your own.
Lorenzo. Nor you nor me, my lord, but both in one,
For I suspect, and the presumption's great,
That by those base confederates in our fault   10
Touching the death of Don Horatio,
We are betrayed to old Hieronimo.
Balthazar. Betrayed, Lorenzo? Tush, it cannot be.
Lorenzo. A guilty conscience, urgèd with the thought
Of former evils, easily cannot err.   15
I am persuaded, and dissuade me not,
That all's revealèd to Hieronimo.
And therefore know that I have cast it thus—

[Enter Page.]

But here's the page. How now, what news with thee?
Page. My lord, Serberine is slain.   20
Balthazar. Who? Serberine, my man?
Page. Your highness' man, my lord.
Lorenzo. Speak, page, who murdered him?

III.iv.2.] Fear of being too late to avert our mishaps.
    3.] What evil is it that you mean, that we don't even suspect the existence of?
    8.] Neither you nor I alone, my lord, but both of us together.
    10–11.] that by those rascally fellows (Pedringano and Serberine) who assisted us in our crime having to do with the death of Don Horatio.
    14–15.] My guilty conscience, the pricking of which is made more intense by my awareness of former crimes, cannot be mistaken.
    18. *cast*] contrived (as at III.ii.100).

Page. He that is apprehended for the fact.

Lorenzo. Who?   25

Page. Pedringano.

Balthazar. Is Serberine slain, that loved his lord so well?
    Injurious villain, murderer of his friend!

Lorenzo. Hath Pedringano murdered Serberine?
    My lord, let me entreat you to take the pains   30
    To exasperate and hasten his revenge
    With your complaints unto my lord the King.
    This their dissension breeds a greater doubt.

Balthazar. Assure thee, Don Lorenzo, he shall die,
    Or else his highness hardly shall deny.   35
    Meanwhile, I'll haste the marshal-sessions;
    For die he shall for this his damnèd deed.   *More revenge*

                           Exit BALTHAZAR.

Lorenzo. Why so, this fits our former policy,
    And thus experience bids the wise to deal.
    I lay the plot, he prosecutes the point;   40
    I set the trap, he breaks the worthless twigs
    And sees not that wherewith the bird was limed.
    Thus hopeful men, that mean to hold their own,

---

24. *fact*] crime, evil deed.

31. *exasperate*] make harsh.
his revenge] revenge upon him.

33.] This evident quarrel between Pedringano and Serberine increases my fear (that we will betrayed). (Lorenzo of course set Pedringano on to murder Serberine, but pretends to be innocent of the knowledge in order to give Balthazar a clear motive for accusing Pedringano of treachery against Balthazar's servant.)

35. *hardly shall deny*] will show harshness in denying me, or, will refuse only with the greatest difficulty.

36. *the marshal-sessions*] the court sessions presided over by the Knight Marshal, Hieronimo.

38. *our former policy*] the cunning I have been using. (Lorenzo gloats to himself and the audience; the Page, even though Lorenzo uses him in his villainy, is hardly the person to whom Lorenzo is about to confess himself. The Page stands respectfully aside until he is called upon at l. 50.)

40. *prosecutes the point*] carries out the doing of it.

41–2.] i.e. I set the trap; Balthazar takes the bird capture, breaking the twigs as he does so on which the sticky bird-lime was spread to ensnare the bird, and thus not seeing my cunning in this.

43–4.] i.e. Thus enterprising villains who mean to prosper must put on deceptive appearances even to their closest friends.

Must look like fowlers to their dearest friends.
He runs to kill whom I have holp to catch,   45
And no man knows it was my reaching fatch.
'Tis hard to trust unto a multitude,
Or anyone, in mine opinion,
When men themselves their secrets will reveal.

Enter a Messenger *with a letter.*

Boy!   50
Page. My lord?
Lorenzo. What's he?
Messenger.   I have a letter to your lordship.
Lorenzo. From whence?
Messenger.   From Pedringano that's imprisoned.
                            [*He delivers the letter.*]
Lorenzo. So, he is in prison, then?
Messenger.   Ay, my good lord.
Lorenzo. What would he with us? He writes us here   55
To stand good lord and help him in distress.
Tell him I have his letters, know his mind,
And what we may, let him assure him of.
Fellow, begone. My boy shall follow thee.

                            Exit Messenger.

This works like wax, yet once more try thy wits.   60
Boy, go convey this purse to Pedringano.

                            [*Gives a purse.*]
Thou know'st the prison; closely give it him,
And be advised that none be there about.
Bid him be merry still, but secret;

---

45. *whom I have holp*] the very person I have helped.
46. *reaching fatch*] far-seeing stratagem.
49.] seeing that men are so prone to reveal even their innermost secrets.
50. *Boy!*] The abruptness of this summons confirms that Lorenzo has been talking to himself; now, interrupted by the entrance of an unknown person, Lorenzo bids the Page see who it is. The Messenger doesn't wait for an introduction.
56. *stand good lord*] act the part of protector or patron.
60.] This situation is malleable and can be shaped to my intents, and so, once more, Lorenzo, have your wits about you. (Said to himself, though not necessarily out of the hearing of the Page, whom Lorenzo turns to in the next line.)
62. *closely*] secretly.
63. *be advised*] take care.

And though the marshal-sessions be today,   65
Bid him not doubt of his delivery.
Tell him his pardon is already signed,
And thereon bid him boldly be resolved;
For, were he ready to be turnèd off
(As 'tis my will the uttermost be tried),   70
Thou with his pardon shalt attend him still.
Show him this box, tell him his pardon's in't,

                   [*Gives a box.*]

But open't not, an if thou lov'st thy life,
But let him wisely keep his hopes unknown;
He shall not want while Don Lorenzo lives.   75
Away!
Page.   I go, my lord, I run.
Lorenzo. But sirrah, see that this be cleanly done. *Exit* Page.
Now stands our fortune on a tickle point,
And now or never ends Lorenzo's doubts.
One only thing is uneffected yet,   80
And that's to see the executioner.
But to what end? I list not trust the air
With utterance of our pretence therein,
For fear the privy whisp'ring of the wind
Convey our words amongst unfriendly ears,   85
That lie too open to advantages.
E quel che voglio io, nessun lo sa;
Intendo io, quel mi basterà.   *Exit.*

---

69. *turnèd off*] hanged.

70.] Lorenzo's parenthetical statement is perfectly ambiguous: he will try his uttermost to save Pedringano from hanging or to make sure that the sentence is carried out.

73. *an if*] if.

75.] Again, Lorenzo speaks ambiguously: Pedringano 'will be taken care of' and will be in a situation of having no further desires, while Lorenzo will be the one who lives.

77. *cleanly*] efficiently.

78. *tickle*] delicately balanced, ticklish.

79. *ends Lorenzo's doubts*] Lorenzo's worries end.

81. *see*] The 1592 edition's 'see' is perhaps a misprint for 'fee'.

82. *list not*] have no wish to.

83. *our pretence*] my intention.

86. *advantages*] opportunities for taking advantage.

87-8.] And what I want, no one knows; I understand, and that's enough for me. (Italian.)

[III. v]

Enter Boy *with the box.*

Page. My master hath forbidden me to look in this box, and
by my troth 'tis likely, if he had not warned me, I should
not have had so much idle time; for we men's-kind in our
minority are like women in their uncertainty: that they
are most forbidden, they will soonest attempt; so I now.   5
[*Opens the box.*] By my bare honesty, here's nothing but
the bare empty box. Were it not sin against secrecy, I
would say it were a piece of gentlemanlike knavery. I
must go to Pedringano, and tell him his pardon is in this
box; nay, I would have sworn it, had I not seen the   10
contrary. I cannot choose but smile to think how the
villain will flout the gallows, scorn the audience, and
descant on the hangman, and all presuming of his pardon
from hence. Will 't not be an odd jest, for me to stand and
grace every jest he makes, pointing my finger at this box,   15
as who would say, 'Mock on, here's thy warrant.' Is't not
a scurvy jest, that a man should jest himself to death?
Alas, poor Pedringano, I am in a sort sorry for thee, but
if I should be hanged with thee, I cannot weep.   *Exit.*

[III. vi]

Enter HIERONIMO *and the* Deputy.

Hieronimo. Thus must we toil in other men's extremes,
    That know not how to remedy our own,

III.v.2–3. *if . . . time*] i.e. if he hadn't told me not to, I wouldn't have taken
the time to bother.
    4. *that*] that which.
    6–7. *bare . . . bare*] simple . . . mere, unadorned.
    13. *descant*] warble, comment.
    16. *as who would say*] as if to say.
    17. *scurvy*] shabby. (Literally, scabby.)
    18. *in a sort*] in a way.
    19. *if*] even if. The Page makes playfully literal use of a conventional
phrase, as in 'I'll be hanged if I know', meaning, 'Even if my life depended
on it I couldn't tell you.'

III.vi.] Hieronimo is presiding over the marshal-sessions.
    0.1. Deputy] the official title of the assistant to the Knight Marshal.

And do them justice, when unjustly we,
For all our wrongs, can compass no redress.
But shall I never live to see the day   5
That I may come, by justice of the heavens,
To know the cause that may my cares allay?
This toils my body, this consumeth age,
That only I to all men just must be,
And neither gods nor men be just to me.   *unfair*   10
Deputy. Worthy Hieronimo, your office asks
  A care to punish such as do transgress.
Hieronimo. So is't my duty to regard his death
  Who, when he lived, deserved my dearest blood.
  But come, for that we came for, let's begin,   15
  For here lies that which bids me to be gone.

                  Enter Officers [*including a Hangman*],
                         Boy *and* PEDRINGANO,
                    with a letter in his hand, bound.

Deputy. Bring forth the prisoner, for the court is set.
Pedringano. Gramercy, boy, but it was time to come,
  For I had written to my lord anew
  A nearer matter that concerneth him,   20
  For fear his lordship had forgotten me;
  But sith he hath remembered me so well—
  Come, come, come on, when shall we to this gear?
Hieronimo. Stand forth, thou monster, murderer of men,
  And here, for satisfaction of the world,   25

---

4. *compass*] achieve.
13. *duty*] sacred duty to revenge a slaughtered son or other kin (as distinguished from the duties or 'office' of a judge).
regard his death] show concern for the death of him, Horatio.
14.] who, even when he lived, deserved that I be ready to share my dearest blood for him, and deserved the good blood or lineage of his descent from me.
15. *that*] that which.
16. *here*] i.e. in my heart or in my head. (The actor gestures, perhaps indicating the bloody handkerchief worn near his heart.)
16.1. a Hangman] The Hangman brings a rope with him (see l. 47). In addition, either here or at the start of the scene, some scaffolding may be brought on; see ll. 50 ff. Compare the presumed use of a stage trellis or 'arbour' for Horatio's hanging in II.iv.
18. *Gramercy*] thanks. (French *grand merci*.)
23. *to this gear*] get on to the business at hand.

Confess thy folly and repent thy fault,
For there's thy place of execution.
Pedringano. This is short work. Well, to your marshalship
First I confess, nor fear I death therefore,
I am the man, 'twas I slew Serberine.   30
But sir, then you think this shall be the place
Where we shall satisfy you for this gear?
Deputy. Ay, Pedringano.
Pedringano.   Now I think not so.
Hieronimo. Peace, impudent, for thou shalt find it so.
For blood with blood shall, while I sit as judge,   35
Be satisfied, and the law discharged;
And though myself cannot receive the like,
Yet will I see that others have their right.
Dispatch! The fault's approvèd and confessed,
And by our law he is condemned to die.   40
Hangman. Come on, sir, are you ready?
Pedringano. To do what, my fine officious knave?
Hangman. To go to this gear.
Pedringano. O sir, you are too forward. Thou wouldst fain
furnish me with a halter, to disfurnish me of my habit; so   45
I should go out of this gear, my raiment, into that gear,
the rope. But, hangman, now I spy your knavery, I'll not
change without boot, that's flat.
Hangman. Come, sir.
Pedringano. So then, I must up?   50
Hangman. No remedy.
Pedringano. Yes, but there shall be for my coming down.

---

32. *for this gear*] for this behaviour, deed, or action.
39. *approvèd*] proved.
43. *to this gear*] The word gear, variously used in ll. 23 and 32, now takes on the added meaning of 'the hangman's equipment'. Pedringano, taking up the gambit in a bantering spirit, applies *gear* to 'raiment' or 'clothing' as well as to the 'rope' (l. 47).
45. *disfurnish . . . habit*] Pedringano refers jestingly to the custom which granted the hangman his victim's clothes.
47. *now*] now that.
48. *without boot*] more desperate punning to fit Pedringano's bravado: (*a*) without some tangible benefit (*boot* means 'advantage, profit, something thrown into the bargain'); (*b*) and thus lose my boots.

Hangman. Indeed, here's a remedy for that.

Pedringano. How? Be turned off?

Hangman. Ay, truly. Come, are you ready? I pray, sir, 55
   dispatch; the day goes away.

Pedringano. What, do you hang by the hour? If you do, I may
   chance to break your old custom.

Hangman. Faith, you have reason, for I am like to break your
   young neck. 60

Pedringano. Dost thou mock me, hangman? Pray God I be
   not preserved to break your knave's pate for this!

Hangman. Alas, sir, you are a foot too low to reach it, and I
   hope you will never grow so high while I am in the office.

Pedringano. Sirrah, dost see yonder boy with the box in his 65
   hand?

Hangman. What, he that points to it with his finger?

Pedringano. Ay, that companion.

Hangman. I know him not, but what of him?

Pedringano. Dost thou think to live till his old doublet will 70
   make thee a new truss?

Hangman. Ay, and many a fair year after, to truss up many
   an honester man than either thou or he.

Pedringano. What hath he in his box, as thou think'st?

Hangman. Faith, I cannot tell, nor I care not greatly. 75
   Methinks you should rather hearken to your soul's
   health.

---

54. *turned off*] Compare III.iv.69 and n.

59. *you have reason*] you are right.

like] likely.

break] The Hangman answers Pedringano's 'break [i.e. violate] your old
custom' (l. 58) with a more literal meaning of 'break in two'. Pedringano
retorts with a third sense of break, to hit over the head (l. 62).

64. *grow so high*] (*a*) put on another foot's growth and thus be as tall as me;
(*b*) insolently aspire. Pedringano is perhaps played by a boy actor, or at least
a young one, shorter than the Hangman.

68. *companion*] fellow.

70. *doublet*] waistcoat.

71. *truss*] close-fitting body-garment or jacket (again alluding to the custom of granting the hangman the victim's clothes, as at l. 45 and n.). The
Hangman fires back with *to truss* in the sense of 'to hang' (l. 72).

75. *Faith*] in good faith, by my troth.

Pedringano. Why, sirrah hangman? I take it, that that is good
    for the body is likewise good for the soul; and it may be,
    in that box is balm for both.   80

Hangman. Well, thou art even the merriest piece of man's
    flesh that e'er groaned at my office door.

Pedringano. Is your roguery become an office, with a knave's
    name?

Hangman. Ay, and that shall all they witness that see you   85
    seal it with a thief's name.

Pedringano. I prithee request this good company to pray with
    me.

Hangman. Ay, marry sir, this is a good motion. My masters,
    you see here's a good fellow.   90

Pedringano. Nay, nay, now I remember me, let them alone till
    some other time, for now I have no great need.

Hieronimo. I have not seen a wretch so impudent!
    O monstrous times, where murder's set so light,
    And where the soul, that should be shrined in heaven,   95
    Solely delights in interdicted things,
    Still wand'ring in the thorny passages
    That intercepts itself of happiness.
    Murder, O bloody monster—God forbid
    A fault so foul should scape unpunishèd!   100
    Dispatch, and see this execution done.
    This makes me to remember thee, my son.

                                         Exit HIERONIMO.

Pedringano. Nay, soft, no haste.

Deputy. Why, wherefore stay you? Have you hope of life?

Pedringano. Why, ay.   105

Hangman. As how?

Pedringano. Why, rascal, by my pardon from the King.

---

78. *that that*] that which.
81–2. *piece of man's flesh*] specimen of humanity.
83–4. *with a knave's name*] (a) in the name of knavery; (b) with the name
of a knave (i.e. you, the Hangman) attached to it. Pedringano mocks the idea
that a base occupation like hanging should be called an 'office'.
86. *seal it*] attest to it (by being hanged).
89. *motion*] proposal.
96. *interdicted*] forbidden.
98.] that cut the soul off from eternal happiness.

Hangman. Stand you on that? Then you shall off with this.
                                            He turns him off.
Deputy. So, executioner; convey him hence,
     But let his body be unburièd.   110
     Let not the earth be chokèd or infect
     With that which heaven contemns and men neglect.
                                            Exeunt.

[III. vii]

                    Enter HIERONIMO.

Hieronimo. Where shall I run to breathe abroad my woes—
     My woes, whose weight hath wearièd the earth?
     Or mine exclaims, that have surcharged the air
     With ceaseless plaints for my deceasèd son?
     The blust'ring winds, conspiring with my words,   5
     At my lament have moved the leafless trees,
     Disrobed the meadows of their flowered green,
     Made mountains marsh with spring-tides of my tears,
     And broken through the brazen gates of hell.
     Yet still tormented is my tortured soul   10
     With broken sighs and restless passions,
     That wingèd mount, and, hovering in the air,
     Beat at the windows of the brightest heavens,
     Soliciting for justice and revenge.
     But they are placed in those empyreal heights   15

108.] The Hangman appropriately ends with a jest: if you hope to stand
[i.e. rely on] the King's pardon, you'll not be standing any longer on this
platform.
     111. *infect*] infected.
     112. *contemns*] despises.
     neglect] shun, leave unattended.

III.vii.1. *breathe abroad*] give expression to.
     3. *exclaims*] exclamations, outcries.
     4. *plaints*] lamentations.
     12. *That wingèd mount*] that mount on wings.
     15. *they*] the gods (who should hear Hieronimo's cries).
     empyreal] pertaining to the sphere of fire or highest heaven, the empyrean.
The 1592 edition's *imperiall* is a common spelling, probably also with conno-
tations of majesty.

Where, countermured with walls of diamond,
I find the place impregnable, and they
Resist my woes, and give my words no way.

Enter Hangman *with a letter.*

Hangman. O lord, sir, God bless you, sir, the man, sir,
    Petergade, sir, he that was so full of merry conceits—   20
Hieronimo. Well, what of him?
Hangman. O lord, sir, he went the wrong way; the fellow had
    a fair commission to the contrary. Sir, here is his pass-
    port; I pray you, sir, we have done him wrong.
Hieronimo. I warrant thee, give it me.   [*Takes the letter.*]   25
Hangman. You will stand between the gallows and me?
Hieronimo. Ay, ay.
Hangman. I thank your lord-worship.   *Exit* Hangman.
Hieronimo. And yet, though somewhat nearer me concerns,
    I will, to ease the grief that I sustain,   30
    Take truce with sorrow while I read on this.
    'My lord, I write, as mine extremes required,
    That you would labour my delivery.
    If you neglect, my life is desperate,
    And in my death I shall reveal the troth.   35
    You know, my lord, I slew him for your sake;
    And was confederate with the prince and you,
    Won by rewards and hopeful promises.
    I holp to murder Don Horatio, too.'
    Holp he to murder mine Horatio?   40
    An actor in th' accursèd tragedy

---

16. *countermured*] doubly walled.
20. *conceits*] fanciful notions, whims.
23. *fair commission*] properly written authority.
23–4. *passport*] authorization to be freed.
26.] i.e. do I have your assurance that you'll protect me from hanging for having executed a man who had a letter authorizing him to do what he had done?
28. *lord-worship*] an unusual form of polite address, but clear enough in meaning: 'I thank you lordship, your worship.'
29.] And yet, though more pressing matters concern me more dearly.
32. *required*] have required.
33. *labour*] work to achieve.
36. *him*] Serberine.

Wast thou, Lorenzo, Balthazar, and thou,
Of whom my son, my son, deserved so well?
What have I heard, what have mine eyes beheld?
O sacred heavens, may it come to pass   45
That such a monstrous and detested deed,
So closely smothered and so long concealed,
Shall thus by this be vengèd or revealed?
Now see I what I durst not then suspect,
That Bel-imperia's letter was not feigned,   50
Nor feignèd she, though falsely they have wronged
Both her, myself, Horatio and themselves.
Now may I make compare, 'twixt hers and this,
Of every accident; I ne'er could find
Till now, and now I feelingly perceive,   55
They did what heaven unpunished would not leave.
O false Lorenzo, are these thy flattering looks?
Is this the honour that thou didst my son?
And Balthazar, bane to thy soul and me,
Was this the ransom he reserved thee for?   60
Woe to the cause of these constrainèd wars,
Woe to thy baseness and captivity,
Woe to thy birth, thy body and thy soul,
Thy cursèd father, and thy conquered self!
And banned with bitter execrations be   65
The day and place where he did pity thee!
But wherefore waste I mine unfruitful words,
When naught but blood will satisfy my woes?
I will go plain me to my lord the King,
And cry aloud for justice through the court,   70

---

48. *by this*] by the letter.
50. *was not feigned*] i.e. was truly written by her.
51-2.] nor did she lie in what she wrote, despite the attempts of Lorenzo and Balthazar to malign her and all of us.
53-6.] Now, from the two letters (Bel-imperia's and Pedringano's), I can piece together the whole occurrence. I could never satisfy myself before, though now it is brought right home to me, that these men committed the murder—which heaven was bound to bring to light and is sure to punish.
60. *reserved*] spared, saved from death.
65. *banned*] cursed.
66. *where . . . thee*] where Horatio spared your life.
69. *plain me*] complain.

Wearing the flints with these my withered feet,
And either purchase justice by entreats
Or tire them all with my revenging threats.   *Exit.*

[III. viii]

Enter ISABELLA *and her* Maid.

Isabella. So that you say this herb will purge the eye,
  And this the head?
  Ah, but none of them will purge the heart.
  No, there's no medicine left for my disease,
  Nor any physic to recure the dead.   *She runs lunatic.*   5
  Horatio! O where's Horatio?
Maid. Good madam, affright not thus yourself
  With outrage for your son Horatio.
  He sleeps in quiet in the Elysian fields.
Isabella. Why, did I not give you gowns and goodly things,   10
  Bought you a whistle and a whipstalk too,
  To be revengèd on their villainies?
Maid. Madam, these humours do torment my soul.
Isabella. My soul? Poor soul, thou talks of things
  Thou know'st not what. My soul hath silver wings,   15
  That mounts me up unto the highest heavens,
  To heaven—ay, there sits my Horatio,
  Backed with a troop of fiery cherubins,
  Dancing about his newly-healèd wounds,
  Singing sweet hymns and chanting heavenly notes,   20
  Rare harmony to greet his innocence,

---

71. *Wearing the flints*] wearing out the flagstones.
73. *tire*] (*a*) weary; (*b*) tear apart their flesh, as a hawk tears with its beak.

III.viii.5. *recure*] restore to health.
8. *outrage*] passionate behaviour, outcry.
11. *whipstalk*] whipstock, handle of a whip.
14. *talks*] talk'st.
16. *mounts*] mount.
18. *Backed with*] supported and comforted by.
fiery] i.e. dwelling in the sphere of fire of highest heaven, the empyrean;
see III.vii.15 and n.
21. *greet*] acclaim, honour, salute (not 'welcome').

That died, ay, died, a mirror in our days.
But say, where shall I find the men, the murderers,
That slew Horatio? Whither shall I run
To find them out that murdèred my son?   *Exeunt.*   25

[III. ix]

BEL-IMPERIA *at a window.*

Bel-imperia. What means this outrage that is offered me?
Why am I thus sequestered from the court?
No notice? Shall I not know the cause
Of this my secret and suspicious ills?
Accursèd brother, unkind murderer,   5
Why bends thou thus thy mind to martyr me?
Hieronimo, why writ I of thy wrongs,
Or why art thou so slack in thy revenge?
Andrea, O Andrea, that thou sawest
Me for thy friend Horatio handled thus,   10
And him for me thus causeless murderèd!
Well, force perforce, I must constrain myself

---

22. *mirror*] paragon, model of excellence.
25.S.D. Exeunt] Isabella runs madly offstage, the Maid in pursuit of her.

III.ix.0.1. at a window] at an upper level in the playhouse, in the gallery
over the main stage. In III.ii, Bel-imperia drops a letter apparently from a
window in her father's house, to be found by Hieronimo. Conceivably she is
still there, confined to her rooms, but the text also allows the interpretation
that she may have been moved to a another location; see l. 2 and III.x.31 and
60.
    2. *sequestered from the court*] kept in seclusion, allowed to see no one—on
Lorenzo's orders (see ll. 5–6), not with the Duke of Castile's knowledge (see
III.x.13–14).
    3. *notice*] information.
    6. *Why bends thou thus*] why do you thus apply.
    7.] Hieronimo, why do you think I wrote to tell you of the wrongs done
you.
    9. *that*] would that. (Bel-imperia's longing to have Andrea know of the
outrages she and Horatio have suffered for each other is ironically intensified
in the theatre by the presence of Andrea's silent yet infuriated ghost; see
III.xv.)
    12. *force perforce*] of necessity.

To patience, and apply me to the time,
Till heaven, as I have hoped, shall set me free.

Enter CHRISTOPHIL.

Christophil. Come, Madam Bel-imperia, this may not be.   15
                                        Exeunt.

[III. x]

Enter LORENZO, BALTHAZAR, *and the* Page.

Lorenzo. Boy, talk no further; thus far things go well.
    Thou art assurèd that thou sawest him dead?
Page. Or else, my lord, I live not.
Lorenzo.   That's enough.
    As for his resolution in his end,
    Leave that to him with whom he sojourns now.   5
    Here, take my ring, and give it Christophil,
    And bid him let my sister be enlarged,
    And bring her hither straight.   *Exit* Page.
    This that I did was for a policy
    To smooth and keep the murder secret,   10
    Which as a nine-days' wonder being o'er-blown,
    My gentle sister will I now enlarge.
Balthazar. And time, Lorenzo, for my lord the duke,
    You heard, enquirèd for her yesternight.

---

13. *apply . . . time*] conform myself to the reality of the situation.
14.1. Enter *CHRISTOPHIL*] presumably 'above'. It would be too awkward for this custodian of Bel-imperia to enter on the main stage for his single line.

III.x. Lorenzo has come to the place where Bel-imperia is concealed, either in the Duke of Castile's house or at a more removed location; see note at III.ix.o.1.
4–5.] i.e. Regarding the final disposition of Pedringano's soul as he is dissolved into the elements, leave that to God or the devil—more likely the latter. (Or, *resolution* may mean 'courage'.)
7. *enlarged*] released from confinement.
9. *policy*] stratagem.
10. *smooth*] smooth things over.
11.] which now has blown over, like many a nine-days' wonder.
12. *gentle*] well born.
13. *time*] in good time.

Lorenzo. Why, and, my lord, I hope you heard me say   15
    Sufficient reason why she kept away.
    But that's all one. My lord, you love her?
Balthazar.   Ay.
Lorenzo. Then in your love beware, deal cunningly,
    Salve all suspicions, only soothe me up;
    And if she hap to stand on terms with us,   20
    As for her sweetheart, and concealment so,
    Jest with her gently; under feignèd jest
    Are things concealed that else would breed unrest.
    But here she comes.

                    Enter BEL-IMPERIA.

                    Now, sister—

Bel-imperia.   Sister? No,
    Thou art no brother, but an enemy!   25
    Else wouldst thou not have used thy sister so.
    First, to affright me with thy weapons drawn,
    And with extremes abuse my company;
    And then to hurry me, like whirlwind's rage,
    Amidst a crew of thy confederates,   30
    And clap me up where none might come at me,
    Nor I at any to reveal my wrongs.
    What madding fury did possess thy wits?
    Or wherein is't that I offended thee?
Lorenzo. Advise you better, Bel-imperia,   35
    For I have done you no disparagement,
    Unless, by more discretion than deserved,
    I sought to save your honour and mine own.
Bel-imperia. Mine honour! Why, Lorenzo, wherein is't
    That I neglect my reputation so,   40
    As you, or any, need to rescue it?

---

17. *that's all one*] never mind that.
19.] smooth over all suspicions and above all back me up in what I say.
20. *stand on terms*] insist on conditions, make difficulties.
28. *company*] companion.
31. *clap*] brusquely lock.
37. *Unless*] unless it were that.

Lorenzo. His highness and my father were resolved
        To come confer with old Hieronimo,
        Concerning certain matters of estate
        That by the viceroy was determinèd.   45
Bel-imperia. And wherein was mine honour touched in that?
Balthazar. Have patience, Bel-imperia; hear the rest.
Lorenzo. Me next in sight as messenger they sent,
        To give him notice that they were so nigh.
        Now when I came, consorted with the prince,   50
        And unexpected in an arbour there
        Found Bel-imperia with Horatio—
Bel-imperia. How then?
Lorenzo. Why then, remembering that old disgrace
        Which you for Don Andrea had endured,   55
        And now were likely longer to sustain,
        By being found so meanly accompanied,
        Thought rather, for I knew no readier mean,
        To thrust Horatio forth my father's way.
Balthazar. And carry you obscurely somewhere else,   60
        Lest that his highness should have found you there.
Bel-imperia. Even so, my lord? And you are witness
        That this is true which he entreateth of?
        You, gentle brother, forged this for my sake,

---

44. *estate*] state. The proposed marriage of Bel-imperia to Balthazar (of which, as yet, she has heard nothing) would be a state marriage that would also involve the settlement of estates. The Viceroy of Portugal is therefore an interested party. Lorenzo pretends that the King and his counsellors came to Hieronimo at his house to consult on legal matters appertaining.

48. *next in sight*] standing nearby.

49. *him*] Hieronimo.

50. *consorted with*] in the company of.

54. *that old disgrace*] the disgrace of Bel-imperia's being whispered to be Andrea's lover.

56.] A liaison with Horatio, Lorenzo insists, was all too likely and would have worsened the disgrace to Bel-imperia's reputation.

57. *meanly*] by one of comparatively low social station.

59. *forth*] out of. Lorenzo pretends he wanted to get Horatio out of sight before the Duke of Castile and the King arrived, at which point the disgrace of Bel-imperia's sexual behaviour would be open. As instructed, Balthazar backs him up.

63. *entreateth of*] discusses.

64. *gentle*] well born, as at l. 12, but with audible irony here.

forged] planned and carried out (with suggestion also of deceit).

And you, my lord, were made his instrument.   65
A work of worth, worthy the noting too!
But what's the cause that you concealed me since?
Lorenzo. Your melancholy, sister, since the news
Of your first favourite Don Andrea's death,
My father's old wrath hath exasperate.   70
Balthazar. And better was't for you, being in disgrace,
To absent yourself and give his fury place.
Bel-imperia. But why had I no notice of his ire?
Lorenzo. That were to add more fuel to your fire,
Who burnt like Etna for Andrea's loss.   75
Bel-imperia. Hath not my father then enquired for me?
Lorenzo. Sister, he hath, and thus excused I thee.
                    He whispereth in her ear.
But Bel-imperia, see the gentle prince.
Look on thy love, behold young Balthazar,
Whose passions by thy presence are increased,   80
And in whose melancholy thou mayst see
Thy hate, his love; thy flight, his following thee.
Bel-imperia. Brother, you are become an orator,
I know not, I, by what experience,
Too politic for me, past all compare,   85
Since last I saw you; but content yourself,
The prince is meditating higher things.
Balthazar. 'Tis of thy beauty then, that conquers kings;
Of those thy tresses, Ariadne's twines,

70.] has intensified our father's long-continuing wrath.

72. *place*] full scope.

75. *Who burnt like Etna*] you who burned like the erupting Mount Etna in Sicily.

77.1.] The audience presumably understands that Lorenzo whispers some indelicacy by way of his having excused her absence, or this stage business would have no point.

81–2.] i.e. your scorn and avoidance of him explain his melancholy and amorous pursuit.

86. *content yourself*] be assured. Don't read so much into Balthazar's behaviour.

89–90.] i.e. I am meditating on your beautiful hair, as precious as the thread given by Ariadne to Theseus to enable him to find his way out of King Minos' labyrinth, but which paradoxically in my case has made me your prisoner in love. (Or Kyd may have confused Ariadne with Arachne, the woman skilled in weaving whom Athene defeated in a contest and then

    Wherewith my liberty thou hast surprised;   90
    Of that thine ivory front, my sorrow's map,
    Wherein I see no haven to rest my hope.
Bel-imperia. To love, and fear, and both at once, my lord,
    In my conceit, are things of more import
    Than women's wits are to be busied with.   95
Balthazar. 'Tis I that love.
Bel-imperia.   Whom?
Balthazar.   Bel-imperia.
Bel-imperia. But I that fear.
Balthazar.   Whom?
Bel-imperia.   Bel-imperia.
Lorenzo. Fear yourself?
Bel-imperia.   Ay, brother.
Lorenzo.   How?
Bel-imperia.   As those
    That what they love are loath and fear to lose.
Balthazar. Then, fair, let Balthazar your keeper be.   100
Bel-imperia. No, Balthazar doth fear as well as we:
    Et tremulo metui pavidum junxere timorem,
    Et vanum stolidae proditionis opus.   *Exit.*
Lorenzo. Nay, an you argue things so cunningly,
    We'll go continue this discourse at court.   105
Balthazar. Led by the lodestar of her heavenly looks
    Wends poor oppressèd Balthazar,
    As o'er the mountains walks the wanderer,
    Incertain to effect his pilgrimage.   *Exeunt.*

---

transformed into a spider.) Except for the Ariadne reference, the couplet is
derived from a sonnet of Du Bellay. *Surprised* means 'captured'.
   91. *front*] forehead.
my sorrow's map] picture of my sorrow.
   94. *conceit*] conception, opinion.
   99. *loath and fear*] reluctant and fearful.
   102–3.] They joined dismayed dread to quaking fear, a futile deed of
sottish betrayal. (Another medley of classical sayings, suggesting here perhaps the futility of uniting Bel-imperia's fear of loss with Balthazar's fear of
rejection.)
   104. *an*] if.
   106. *lodestar*] star that shows the way, especially the pole star.
   109. *Incertain to effect*] doubtful that he will achieve.

24

[III. xi]

Enter two Portingales, *and* HIERONIMO *meets them.*

First Portuguese. By your leave, sir.
                            [Third Addition; see pp. 133–5]
Hieronimo. Good leave have you. Nay, I pray you go,
    For I'll leave you, if you can leave me, so.
Second Portuguese. Pray you, which is the next way to my lord
    the duke's?
Hieronimo. The next way from me.
First Portuguese.   To his house, we mean.   5
Hieronimo. Oh, hard by, 'tis yon house that you see.
Second Portuguese. You could not tell us if his son were there?
Hieronimo. Who, my lord Lorenzo?
First Portuguese.   Ay, sir.
        He goeth in at one door and comes out at another.
Hieronimo.   Oh, forbear,
    For other talk for us far fitter were.
    But if you be importunate to know   10
    The way to him, and where to find him out,
    Then list to me, and I'll resolve your doubt.
    There is a path upon your left-hand side,
    That leadeth from a guilty conscience
    Unto a forest of distrust and fear,   15
    A darksome place and dangerous to pass;
    There shall you meet with melancholy thoughts,
    Whose baleful humours if you but uphold,
    It will conduct you to despair and death;
    Whose rocky cliffs when you have once beheld,   20

III.xi. The scene takes place in the vicinity of the Duke of Castile's house; see l. 6.
  1. *By your leave*] excuse me.
  4. *next*] nearest.
  5. *The next way from me*] i.e. The best way to come at the duke is to go as far as possible away from me.
  8.S.D. *He goeth . . . another*] This stage action suggests that the First Portuguese gentleman goes into the duke's house and returns, not having found Lorenzo.
  13.] The left-hand path leads to the deepest hell, as at I.i.63 and n.
  18. *uphold*] sustain, continue in.

Within a hugy dale of lasting night,
That, kindled with the world's iniquities,
Doth cast up filthy and detested fumes—
Not far from thence, where murderers have built
A habitation for their cursèd souls,   25
There, in a brazen cauldron fixed by Jove
In his fell wrath upon a sulphur flame,
Yourselves shall find Lorenzo bathing him
In boiling lead and blood of innocents.

First Portuguese. Ha, ha, ha!
Hieronimo.   Ha, ha, ha!   30
    Why, ha, ha, ha! Farewell, good, ha, ha, ha!   *Exit.*
Second Portuguese. Doubtless this man is passing lunatic,
    Or imperfection of his age doth make him dote.
    Come, let's away to seek my lord the duke.

                                        [*Exeunt.*]

[III. xii]

        Enter HIERONIMO *with a poniard in one hand, and
                a rope in the other.*

Hieronimo. Now, sir, perhaps I come and see the King;
    The King sees me, and fain would hear my suit.
    Why, is not this a strange and seld-seen thing,
    That standers-by with toys should strike me mute?
    Go to, I see their shifts, and say no more.   5
    Hieronimo, 'tis time for thee to trudge.

---

21. *hugy*] huge.
28. *him*] himself.
32. *passing*] exceedingly.

III.xii.0.1–2. poniard . . . rope] stock theatrical properties of the would-be
suicide. Hieronimo is at court, waiting to lay his accusations before the King,
as he promised at III.vii.69–73.
    1. *Now, sir*] Hieronimo reasons distractedly with some imaginary inter-
locutor or with himself.
    3. *seld-seen*] seldom-seen.
    4. *toys*] vain triflings. Hieronimo's pleading is drowned out by maliciously
intended court drivel.
    5. *Go to*] an expression of impatience.
    shifts] devices.
    6. *trudge*] move off, get going.

Down by the dale that flows with purple gore
Standeth a fiery tower; there sits a judge
Upon a seat of steel and molten brass,
And 'twixt his teeth he holds a firebrand,   10
That leads unto the lake where hell doth stand.
Away, Hieronimo, to him be gone!
He'll do thee justice for Horatio's death.
Turn down this path, thou shalt be with him straight,
Or this, and then thou need'st not take thy breath.   15
This way, or that way? Soft and fair, not so;
For if I hang or kill myself, let's know
Who will revenge Horatio's murder then?
No, no! Fie, no! Pardon me, I'll none of that.
                    He flings away the dagger and halter.
This way I'll take, and this way comes the King,   20
                    He takes them up again.
And here I'll have a fling at him, that's flat.
And, Balthazar, I'll be with thee to bring,
And thee, Lorenzo! Here's the King, nay, stay,
And here, ay here, there goes the hare away.

          Enter KING, AMBASSADOR, CASTILE *and* LORENZO.

King. Now show, Ambassador, what our viceroy saith.   25
     Hath he received the articles we sent?
Hieronimo. Justice, O justice to Hieronimo!
Lorenzo. Back! Seest thou not the King is busy?
Hieronimo. Oh, is he so?

---

11. *the lake*] the river Avernus, or perhaps Cocytus.

12. *him*] Pluto, monarch of hell.

14–15. *this path . . . Or this*] Hieronimo brandishes the poniard and then
the rope.

15. *and then . . . breath*] and then you need draw the breath of life no
longer.

16. *Soft and fair*] gently, wait a moment.

17. *let's know*] let us stop and ponder.

21.] and here I'll have a go at petitioning the King, that's for certain.

22. *I'll . . . to bring*] i.e. I'll be even with you.

24. *there . . . away*] a proverb suggesting Hieronimo's fear of losing his
opportunity with the King.

25. *our viceroy*] The King of Spain considers the ruler of Portugal to owe
Spain fealty, as the title *viceroy*, 'vice-king', suggests.

King. Who is he that interrupts our business?   30
Hieronimo. Not I. Hieronimo, beware; go by, go by.
Ambassador. Renownèd King, he hath received and read
    Thy kingly proffers and thy promised league,
    And, as a man extremely overjoyed
    To hear his son so princely entertained,   35
    Whose death he had so solemnly bewailed,
    This, for thy further satisfaction
    And kingly love, he kindly lets thee know:
    First, for the marriage of his princely son
    With Bel-imperia, thy beloved niece,   40
    The news are more delightful to his soul
    Than myrrh or incense to the offended heavens.
    In person therefore will he come himself
    To see the marriage rites solemnizèd,
    And, in the presence of the court of Spain,   45
    To knit a sure, inexplicable bond
    Of kingly love and everlasting league
    Betwixt the crowns of Spain and Portingale.
    There will he give his crown to Balthazar,
    And make a queen of Bel-imperia.   50
King. Brother, how like you this our viceroy's love?
Castile. No doubt, my lord, it is an argument
    Of honourable care to keep his friend,
    And wondrous zeal to Balthazar his son;
    Nor am I least indebted to his grace,   55
    That bends his liking to my daughter thus.
Ambassador. Now last, dread lord, here hath his highness sent
    (Although he send not that his son return)
    His ransom due to Don Horatio.
                      [The ransom is brought forward.]
Hieronimo. Horatio? Who calls Horatio?   60

---

    31. *go by*] literally, go aside; i.e. be careful, don't get into trouble.
    42.] i.e. than myrrh or incense would be to the heavens if, for some reason, the gods were offended and needed to be placated by such offerings.
    46. *inexplicable*] indissoluble.
    52. *an argument*] a token, manifestation.
    53. *keep his friend*] i.e. maintain friendship with the King of Spain.
    56. *bends*] directs.
    58.] i.e. Although the ransom was originally meant to procure the release of the viceroy's son Balthazar, the Viceroy sends it now without desiring that Balthazar return, since a royal marriage is in prospect.

King. And well remembered; thank his majesty.
    Here, see it given to Horatio.
Hieronimo. Justice, O justice, justice, gentle King!
King. Who is that? Hieronimo?
Hieronimo. Justice, O justice! O my son, my son,   65
    My son, whom naught can ransom or redeem!
Lorenzo. Hieronimo, you are not well-advised.
Hieronimo. Away, Lorenzo, hinder me no more,
    For thou hast made me bankrupt of my bliss.
    Give me my son! You shall not ransom him.   70
    Away! I'll rip the bowels of the earth,
                    He diggeth with his dagger.
    And ferry over to th'Elysian plains,
    And bring my son to show his deadly wounds.
    Stand from about me!
    I'll make a pickaxe of my poniard,   75
    And here surrender up my marshalship;
    For I'll go marshal up the fiends in hell,
    To be avengèd on you all for this.
King. What means this outrage?
    Will none of you restrain his fury?   80
Hieronimo. Nay, soft and fair; you shall not need to strive.
    Needs must he go that the devils drive.   *Exit.*
King. What accident hath happed Hieronimo?
    I have not seen him to demean him so.
Lorenzo. My gracious lord, he is with extreme pride,   85
    Conceived of young Horatio his son,
    And covetous of having to himself
    The ransom of the young prince Balthazar,
    Distract, and in a manner lunatic.
King. Believe me, nephew, we are sorry for't.   90
    This is the love that fathers bear their sons.
    But gentle brother, go give to him this gold,

---

79. *outrage*] extravagant outburst.
82.] This familiar proverb usually names 'the devil'; Hieronimo's use of the plural 'devils' is a hit at Lorenzo, Balthazar and their allies.
83. *happed Hieronimo*] happened to Hieronimo.
84. *demean him*] conduct himself, behave.
85–9. *he is . . . Distract*] he is out of his wits through an excess of pride in his son Horatio and through coveting for himself the ransom due to Horatio for Balthazar.
91.] i.e. This shows what can come of fathers' love for their sons.

The prince's ransom; let him have his due;
For what he hath, Horatio shall not want.
Haply Hieronimo hath need thereof.   95
Lorenzo. But if he be thus helplessly distract,
   'Tis requisite his office be resigned
   And given to one of more discretion.
King. We shall increase his melancholy so.
   'Tis best that we see further in it first;   100
   Till when, ourself will not exempt the place.
   And brother, now bring in the ambassador,
   That he may be a witness of the match
   'Twixt Balthazar and Bel-imperia,
   And that we may prefix a certain time   105
   Wherein the marriage shall be solemnized,
   That we may have thy lord the viceroy here.
Ambassador. Therein your highness highly shall content
   His majesty, that longs to hear from hence.
King. On then, and hear you, lord ambassador.   *Exeunt.*   110
             [*Fourth Addition; see pp. 135–41*]

[III. xiii]

    Enter HIERONIMO *with a book in his hand.*

Hieronimo. Vindicta mihi!   Biblical
   Ay, heaven will be revenged of every ill,
   Nor will they suffer murder unrepaid.

---

100. *see further in it*] look more carefully into the matter.
101.] Till which time, I will not debar him from the office.
102. *bring in*] i.e. bring along to the ceremony of troth-plight. The Ambassador is already onstage and is not now being summoned. See next note.
105. *prefix*] fix in advance.
110. hear you] i.e. you shall hear the vows pronounced, and your viceroy will accordingly hear from you.

III.xiii.1. Vindicta mihi] Vengeance is mine (Romans xii.19). Since Seneca makes use of this well-known phrase in his *Octavia* ('*Et hoc sat est? . . . haec vindicta debetur mihi?*', 'And is this enough? . . . Is this the vengeance due to me?'), the book that Hieronimo carries may be imagined to be Seneca, even though here his interpretation of *Vindicta mihi* is distinctly biblical. The Bible and Seneca offer Hieronimo sententious and contradictory advice on revenge. See notes 6 and 12–13 below.
3, 4. *they, their*] the heavens.

Then stay, Hieronimo, attend their will,
For mortal men may not appoint their time.   5
Per scelus semper tutum est sceleribus iter.
Strike, and strike home where wrong is offered thee,
For evils unto ills conductors be,
And death's the worst of resolution;
For he that thinks with patience to contend   *take*   10
To quiet life, his life shall easily end.   *action*
Fata si miseros juvant, habes salutem;   *when*
Fata si vitam negant, habes sepulchrum:
If destiny thy miseries do ease,   *wronged*
Then hast thou health, and happy shalt thou be.   15
If destiny deny thee life, Hieronimo,
Yet shalt thou be assurèd of a tomb;
If neither, yet let this thy comfort be,
Heaven covereth him that hath no burial.
And to conclude, I will revenge his death!   20
But how? Not as the vulgar wits of men,
With open, but inevitable ills,
As by a secret, yet a certain mean,
Which under kindship will be cloakèd best.
Wise men will take their opportunity,   25
Closely and safely fitting things to time;

6.] Adapted from Seneca, *Agamemnon*, 115: '*per scelera semper sceleribus tutum est iter*', 'The safe way for crime is always through crime.' Hieronimo ponders the likelihood that Lorenzo will seek to cover up his murder of Horatio by attempting to kill Hieronimo also. Distraught, Hieronimo vacillates between patient submission to the will of the heavens (ll. 1–5) and desire for violent revenge. The debate continues in what follows.

7. *home*] all the way.

8–11.] for evil only leads to still further ill, and death is the worst thing that can follow from a brave resolution; conversely, anyone who hopes with patience to persevere in living quietly will die at peace.

12–13.] Hieronimo gives the sense of these lines from Seneca's *Troades*, 510–12, in ll. 14–15. Seneca, the great Stoic philosopher, praises stoical contentment here, but is also an authority for revenge (l. 6).

19.] a proverbial saying found in Lucan, *Pharsalia*, VII.819.

20.] Hieronimo's conclusion is, to say the least, abrupt, since he has just been reflecting that destiny and the heavens will provide.

21–4. *Not . . . best*] Not as men of ordinary intelligence devise, by open violence and the inevitable ill consequences therefrom, but by secret and surefire means, best hidden under the cloak of pretended kindness.

But in extremes advantage hath no time,
And therefore all times fit not for revenge.
Thus therefore will I rest me in unrest,
Dissembling quiet in unquietness,   30
Not seeming that I know their villainies,
That my simplicity may make them think
That ignorantly I will let all slip;
For ignorance, I wot, and well they know,
Remedium malorum iners est.   35
Nor aught avails it me to menace them,
Who, as a wintry storm upon a plain,
Will bear me down with their nobility.
No, no, Hieronimo, thou must enjoin
Thine eyes to observation, and thy tongue   40
To milder speeches than thy spirit affords,
Thy heart to patience, and thy hands to rest,
Thy cap to courtesy, and thy knee to bow,
Till to revenge thou know, when, where, and how.
                                    A noise within.
How now, what noise? What coil is that you keep?   45

                Enter a Servant.

Servant. Here are a sort of poor petitioners,
     That are importunate, an it shall please you, sir,
     That you should plead their cases to the King.
Hieronimo. That I should plead their several actions?
     Why, let them enter, and let me see them.   50

            Enter three Citizens *and an* Old Man.

27–8.] Since situations of extremity do not allow one to wait for favour-
able *advantage* or opportunity, one must consider that not all times are
appropriate for revenge.

32. *simplicity*] here, a guise of naivety.

35.] is an idle remedy for ills (adapted from Seneca, *Oedipus*, 515).

38. *nobility*] seniority in title.

43.] Removing the cap and bowing the knee are gestures of *courtesy* toward
those of higher rank.

45.] *What . . . keep?*] What is all this fuss about?

46. *sort*] group, gathering.

47. *an*] if.

49. *several actions*] various individual petitions.

First Citizen. [*To his companions*] So I tell you this: for learning
    and for law
    There's not any advocate in Spain
    That can prevail, or will take half the pain
    That he will, in pursuit of equity.
Hieronimo. Come near, you men that thus importune me.   55
    [*Aside.*] Now must I bear a face of gravity,
    For thus I used, before my marshalship,
    To plead in causes as corregidor.—
    Come on, sirs, what's the matter?
Second Citizen.   Sir, an action.
Hieronimo. Of battery?
First Citizen.   Mine of debt.
Hieronimo.   Give place.   60
Second Citizen. No sir, mine is an action of the case.
Third Citizen. Mine an *ejectione firmae* by a lease.
Hieronimo. Content you, sirs. Are you determinèd
    That I should plead your several actions?
First Citizen. Ay, sir, and here's my declaration.   65
Second Citizen. And here is my bond.
Third Citizen.   And here is my lease.
                    They give him papers.
Hieronimo. But wherefore stands yon silly man so mute,
    With mournful eyes and hands to heaven upreared?
    Come hither, father. Let me know thy cause.
Senex. O worthy sir, my cause but slightly known   70
    May move the hearts of warlike Myrmidons
    And melt the Corsic rocks with ruthful tears.

---

53. *pain*] pains.
58. *corregidor*] properly, the chief magistrate of a Spanish town, but the title was used with some latitude by Elizabethan writers and here obviously means 'advocate'.
61. *action of the case*] a plea requiring a special writ because it does not fall within the limited jurisdiction of the Common Pleas.
62. ejectione firmae] a writ to eject a tenant from his holding before the expiration of his lease.
67. *silly*] poor, to be pitied.
69. *father*] old man. *Senex* has the same meaning.
71. *Myrmidons*] Achilles' warriors in the *Iliad* were renowned for their fierceness; see I.i.48–9 and n.
72. *Corsic rocks*] rocks of Corsica (from Seneca's *Octavia*, 382).

Hieronimo. Say, father, tell me what's thy suit?
Senex. No sir, could my woes
    Give way unto my most distressful words,   75
    Then should I not in paper, as you see,
    With ink bewray what blood began in me.
Hieronimo. What's here? 'The humble supplication
    Of Don Bazulto for his murdered son.'
Senex. Ay, sir.
Hieronimo.   No sir, it was my murdered son,   80
    O my son, my son, O my son Horatio!
    But mine, or thine, Bazulto, be content.
    Here, take my handkerchief and wipe thine eyes,
    Whiles wretched I in thy mishaps may see
    The lively portrait of my dying self.   85
                    He draweth out a bloody napkin.
    O no, not this! Horatio, this was thine.
    And when I dyed it in thy dearest blood,
    This was a token 'twixt thy soul and me
    That of thy death revengèd I should be.
                    [He draws out more objects.]
    But here, take this, and this—what, my purse?—   90
    Ay, this and that, and all of them are thine,
    For all as one are our extremities.
First Citizen. O, see the kindness of Hieronimo!
Second Citizen. This gentleness shows him a gentleman.
Hieronimo. See, see, O see thy shame, Hieronimo,   95
    See here a loving father to his son!
    Behold the sorrows and the sad laments
    That he delivereth for his son's decease!
    If love's effects so strives in lesser things,
    If love enforce such moods in meaner wits,   100
    If love express such power in poor estates,
    Hieronimo, whenas a raging sea,
    Tossed with the wind and tide, o'erturneth then

77.] reveal in writing what violent passion has prompted me to.
100. *meaner wits*] lesser intelligences.
102–5.] Hieronimo compares Bazulto's agitated passion to the stormy
surface of the sea, and his own less demonstrative though deeply felt response to that of deeper water.
102. *whenas*] when.

The upper billows, course of waves to keep,
Whilst lesser waters labour in the deep,   105
Then sham'st thou not, Hieronimo, to neglect
The sweet revenge of thy Horatio?
Though on this earth justice will not be found,
I'll down to hell, and in this passion
Knock at the dismal gates of Pluto's court,   110
Getting by force, as once Alcides did,
A troop of Furies and tormenting hags
To torture Don Lorenzo and the rest.
Yet lest the triple-headed porter should
Deny my passage to the slimy strand,   115
The Thracian poet thou shalt counterfeit:
Come on, old father, be my Orpheus,
And if thou canst no notes upon the harp,
Then sound the burden of thy sore heart's grief,
Till we do gain that Proserpine may grant   120
Revenge on them that murderèd my son.
Then will I rend and tear them thus and thus,
Shivering their limbs in pieces with my teeth.

> *Tear the papers.*

First Citizen. O sir, my declaration!

> *Exit* HIERONIMO *and they after.*

Second Citizen. Save my bond!   125

> *Enter* HIERONIMO.

Save my bond!
Third Citizen. Alas, my lease! It cost me ten pound,
   And you, my lord, have torn the same.
Hieronimo. That cannot be; I gave it never a wound.

---

111. *Alcides*] Hercules, the last of whose labours was to bind Cerberus, the 'triple-headed porter' of Hades mentioned in l. 114.

116. *The Thracian poet*] When Orpheus descended to Hades to bring back his dead wife Eurydice, he played so beautifully that Persephone (Proserpine, l. 120) was induced to grant his request on condition that he not look back at her as she followed him—a condition he fatally forgot. Orpheus was later torn to pieces by Thracian Maenads, in an episode that may be reflected in Hieronimo's talk of rending and tearing his enemies to pieces with his teeth (ll. 122–3).

118. *if thou canst*] if you know.

119. *burden*] (*a*) musical bass or refrain; (*b*) sorrowful load.

Show me one drop of blood fall from the same.   130
How is it possible I should slay it, then?
Tush, no; run after, catch me if you can.

Exeunt all but the Old Man.
BAZULTO *remains till* HIERONIMO *enters again,*
who, staring him in the face, speaks.

Hieronimo. And art thou come, Horatio, from the depth,
    To ask for justice in this upper earth?
    To tell thy father thou art unrevenged,   135
    To wring more tears from Isabella's eyes,
    Whose lights are dimmed with over-long laments?
    Go back, my son; complain to Aeacus,
    For here's no justice. Gentle boy, be gone,
    For justice is exilèd from the earth.   140
    Hieronimo will bear thee company.
    Thy mother cries on righteous Rhadamanth
    For just revenge against the murderers.
Senex. Alas, my lord, whence springs this troubled speech?
Hieronimo. But let me look on my Horatio.   145
    Sweet boy, how art thou changed in death's black shade!
    Had Proserpine no pity on thy youth,
    But suffered thy fair crimson-coloured spring
    With withered winter to be blasted thus?
    Horatio, thou art older than thy father.   150
    Ah, ruthless fate, that favour thus transforms!
Senex. Ah, my good lord, I am not your young son.
Hieronimo. What, not my son? Thou, then, a fury art,
    Sent from the empty kingdom of black night
    To summon me to make appearance   155
    Before grim Minos and just Rhadamanth,
    To plague Hieronimo, that is remiss
    And seeks not vengeance for Horatio's death.
Senex. I am a grievèd man, and not a ghost,
    That came for justice for my murdered son.   160

138, 142, 156. *Aeacus, Rhadamanth, Minos*] The just judges of the underworld who try Andrea's case at I.i.33.
    145. *But*] only.
    149. *blasted*] blighted, nipped with frost.
    151.] Ah, ruthless fate, that thus transforms the countenance!
    157. *that is*] who is.

Hieronimo. Ay, now I know thee, now thou nam'st thy son;
　　Thou art the lively image of my grief;
　　Within thy face, my sorrows I may see.
　　Thy eyes are gummed with tears, thy cheeks are wan,
　　Thy forehead troubled, and thy mutt'ring lips   165
　　Murmur sad words abruptly broken off;
　　By force of windy sighs thy spirit breathes,
　　And all this sorrow riseth for thy son;
　　And selfsame sorrow feel I for my son.
　　Come in, old man, thou shalt to Isabel.   170
　　Lean on my arm; I thee, thou me shalt stay,
　　And thou, and I, and she, will sing a song,
　　Three parts in one, but all of discords framed.—
　　Talk not of cords, but let us now be gone,
　　For with a cord Horatio was slain.   *Exeunt.*   175

[III. xiv]

　　　　　Enter KING of Spain, *the* DUKE, VICEROY, *and*
　　LORENZO, BALTHAZAR, DON PEDRO, *and* BEL-IMPERIA.

King. Go, brother, it is the Duke of Castile's cause;
　　Salute the viceroy in our name.
Castile.　　　　　　　　　I go.
Viceroy. Go forth, Don Pedro, for thy nephew's sake,
　　And greet the Duke of Castile.
Pedro.　　　　　　　　　It shall be so.
King. And now to meet these Portuguese,   5
　　For as we now are, so sometimes were these,
　　Kings and commanders of the western Indies.
　　Welcome, brave viceroy, to the court of Spain,
　　And welcome, all his honourable train.

---

171. *stay*] support.
174. *cords*] Hieronimo has been unhappily reminded of cords (and chords)
by *discords* in l. 173.

III.xiv.] At the Spanish court.
1. *it is . . . cause*] i.e. this royal visit vitally affects the Duke of Castile's
interests as father of the bride-to-be.
3. *for thy nephew's sake*] on behalf of Balthazar, the groom.
6. *sometimes*] sometime, formerly.
7.] Portugal's empire extended into Brazil and parts of Africa, India and
the East Indies, not the West Indies.

'Tis not unknown to us for why you come,   10
Or have so kingly crossed the seas;
Sufficeth it, in this we note the troth
And more than common love you lend to us.
So is it that mine honourable niece
(For it beseems us now that it be known)   15
Already is betrothed to Balthazar,
And by appointment and our condescent
Tomorrow are they to be married.
To this intent we entertain thyself,
Thy followers, their pleasure, and our peace.   20
Speak, men of Portingale, shall it be so?
If ay, say so; if not, say flatly no.
Viceroy. Renownèd king, I come not as thou think'st,
With doubtful followers, unresolvèd men,
But such as have upon thine articles   25
Confirmed thy motion and contented me.
Know, sovereign, I come to solemnize
The marriage of thy belovèd niece,
Fair Bel-imperia, with my Balthazar—
With thee, my son, whom sith I live to see,   30
Here, take my crown; I give it her and thee;
And let me live a solitary life,
In ceaseless prayers,
To think how strangely heaven hath thee preserved.
King. See, brother, see, how nature strives in him!   35
Come, worthy viceroy, and accompany
Thy friend with thine extremities;
A place more private fits this princely mood.

11.] Portugal's proximity to Spain, acknowledged by the Spanish general at I.ii.22–3, would seem to make crossing 'the seas' unnecessary, unless possibly the play is set in Seville, perhaps fifty miles inland from the southern port city of Cadiz.

12. *troth*] faithful loyalty.

17. *condescent*] assent.

20. *their*] i.e. Balthazar's and Bel-imperia's.

26. *motion*] proposal.

34. *strangely*] miraculously.

35. *nature strives in him*] i.e. he weeps.

37. *extremities*] intense emotions.

Viceroy. Or here or where your highness thinks it good.
　　　　　　　Exeunt all but CASTILE *and* LORENZO.
Castile. Nay, stay, Lorenzo, let me talk with you.　　　40
　　Seest thou this entertainment of these kings?
Lorenzo. I do, my lord, and joy to see the same.
Castile. And knowest thou why this meeting is?
Lorenzo. For her, my lord, whom Balthazar doth love,
　　And to confirm their promised marriage.　　　45
Castile. She is thy sister.
Lorenzo.　　　　　　Who, Bel-imperia?
　　Ay, my gracious lord, and this is the day
　　That I have longed so happily to see.
Castile. Thou wouldst be loath that any fault of thine
　　Should intercept her in her happiness.　　　50
Lorenzo. Heavens will not let Lorenzo err so much.
Castile. Why then, Lorenzo, listen to my words:
　　It is suspected, and reported too,
　　That thou, Lorenzo, wrong'st Hieronimo,
　　And in his suits towards his majesty　　　55
　　Still keep'st him back and seeks to cross his suit.
Lorenzo. That I, my lord?
Castile. I tell thee, son, myself have heard it said,
　　When to my sorrow I have been ashamed
　　To answer for thee, though thou art my son.　　　60
　　Lorenzo, know'st thou not the common love
　　And kindness that Hieronimo hath won
　　By his deserts within the court of Spain?
　　Or seest thou not the King my brother's care
　　In his behalf, and to procure his health?　　　65
　　Lorenzo, shouldst thou thwart his passions,
　　And he exclaim against thee to the King,
　　What honour were't in this assembly,
　　Or what a scandal were't among the kings
　　To hear Hieronimo exclaim on thee?　　　70
　　Tell me, and look thou tell me truly too,

---

39. *Or*] either.
50. *intercept*] interrupt, break in upon.
61. *common*] among one and all.
65. *health*] welfare.

Whence grows the ground of this report in court?

Lorenzo. My lord, it lies not in Lorenzo's power
To stop the vulgar, liberal of their tongues.
A small advantage makes a water-breach,   75
And no man lives that long contenteth all.

Castile. Myself have seen thee busy to keep back
Him and his supplications from the King.

Lorenzo. Yourself, my lord, hath seen his passions,
That ill-beseemed the presence of a king,   80
And, for I pitied him in his distress,
I held him thence with kind and courteous words,
As free from malice to Hieronimo
As to my soul, my lord.

Castile. Hieronimo, my son, mistakes thee, then.   85

Lorenzo. My gracious father, believe me, so he doth.
But what's a silly man, distract in mind,
To think upon the murder of his son?
Alas, how easy is it for him to err!
But for his satisfaction and the world's,   90
'Twere good, my lord, that Hieronimo and I
Were reconciled, if he misconster me.

Castile. Lorenzo thou hast said; it shall be so.
Go one of you and call Hieronimo.

Enter BALTHAZAR *and* BEL-IMPERIA.

Balthazar. Come, Bel-imperia, Balthazar's content,   95
My sorrow's ease and sovereign of my bliss,
Sith heaven hath ordained thee to be mine:
Disperse those clouds and melancholy looks,
And clear them up with those thy sun-bright eyes
Wherein my hope and heaven's fair beauty lies.   100

Bel-imperia. My looks, my lord, are fitting for my love,
Which, new begun, can show no brighter yet.

---

74. *the vulgar . . . tongues*] ordinary loose-tongued commoners.
75.] A small break in a dyke eventually leads to a flood; i.e. small faults are
too readily exaggerated by report.
81.] and, because I pitied Hieronimo's madness.
92. *misconster*] interpret wrongly, misconstrue.
93. *thou hast said*] you have spoken wisely.

Balthazar. New-kindled flames should burn as morning sun.
Bel-imperia. But not too fast, lest heat and all be done.
    I see my lord my father.
Balthazar.   Truce, my love,   105
    I will go salute him.
Castile.   Welcome, Balthazar,
    Welcome, brave prince, the pledge of Castile's peace;
    And welcome, Bel-imperia. How now, girl?
    Why com'st thou sadly to salute us thus?
    Content thyself, for I am satisfied.   110
    It is not now as when Andrea lived—
    We have forgotten and forgiven that—
    And thou art gracèd with a happier love.
    But Balthazar, here comes Hieronimo;
    I'll have a word with him.   115

                Enter HIERONIMO *and a* Servant.

Hieronimo. And where's the duke?
Servant.   Yonder.
Hieronimo. [*To himself*]   Even so.
    What new device have they devisèd, trow?
    Pocas palabras, mild as the lamb.
    Is't I will be revenged? No, I am not the man.
Castile. Welcome, Hieronimo.   120
Lorenzo. Welcome, Hieronimo.
Balthazar. Welcome, Hieronimo.
Hieronimo. My lords, I thank you for Horatio.
Castile. Hieronimo, the reason that I sent
    To speak with you is this.
Hieronimo.   What, so short?   125
    Then I'll be gone, I thank you for't.   [*Starts to leave.*]

---

105. *Truce*] i.e. let us call a truce to our parrying in love talk.
107. *the . . . peace*] i.e. through whom Castile (and Spain) commit themselves to peace with Portugal.
117. *trow*] do you think; I wonder. (Hieronimo is musing to himself.)
118. Pocas palabras] few words (Spanish).
119.] Hieronimo assumes his disguise as the mild-mannered and distracted Marshal who wouldn't dream of revenging.
125. *What, so short?*] Hieronimo pretends madly to think that Castile has
finished speaking to him.

Castile. Nay, stay, Hieronimo! Go call him, son.

Lorenzo. Hieronimo, my father craves a word with you.

Hieronimo. With me, sir? Why, my lord, I thought you had
　　done.

Lorenzo. [*Aside*] No, would he had.

Castile.　　　　　　　　　　　Hieronimo, I hear　　　　130
　　You find yourself aggrievèd at my son
　　Because you have not access unto the King,
　　And say 'tis he that intercepts your suits.

Hieronimo. Why, is not this a miserable thing, my lord?

Castile. Hieronimo, I hope you have no cause,　　　135
　　And would be loath that one of your deserts
　　Should once have reason to suspect my son,
　　Considering how I think of you myself.

Hieronimo. Your son Lorenzo? Whom, my noble lord?
　　The hope of Spain, mine honourable friend?　　140
　　Grant me the combat of them, if they dare.
　　　　　　　　　　　　　　　　Draws out his sword.
　　I'll meet him face to face to tell me so.
　　These be the scandalous reports of such
　　As love not me, and hate my lord too much.
　　Should I suspect Lorenzo would prevent　　　145
　　Or cross my suit, that loved my son so well?
　　My lord, I am ashamed it should be said.

Lorenzo. Hieronimo, I never gave you cause.

Hieronimo. My good lord, I know you did not.

Castile.　　　　　　　　　　　There then pause,
　　And for the satisfaction of the world,　　　150
　　Hieronimo, frequent my homely house,
　　The Duke of Castile, Cyprian's ancient seat,
　　And when thou wilt, use me, my son, and it;

---

133. *intercepts*] stands in the way of.

134.] Another whimsical or mad answer of solicitous agreement, that
seems to miss the point of what has been said to him.

136. *And would*] and I would.

139. *Whom?*] We would say 'Who?' The accusative comes implicitly from
l. 137: 'People say that I suspect whom? Your son?'

141. *Grant . . . them*] Allow me to challenge them formally to a duel.

145. *prevent*] forestall.

151. *homely*] hospitable, 'home-like'; humble.

But here, before Prince Balthazar and me,
Embrace each other, and be perfect friends.   155
Hieronimo. Ay, marry, my lord, and shall.
Friends, quoth he? See, I'll be friends with you all,
Specially with you, my lovely lord.
For divers causes it is fit for us
That we be friends; the world is suspicious,   160
And men may think what we imagine not.
Balthazar. Why, this is friendly done, Hieronimo.
Lorenzo. And thus, I hope, old grudges are forgot.
Hieronimo. What else? It were a shame it should not be so.
Castile. Come on, Hieronimo, at my request;   165
Let us entreat your company today.
                              Exeunt [*all but* HIERONIMO].
Hieronimo. Your lordship's to command.—Pha! keep your
way.
Chi mi fa più carezze che non suole,
Tradito mi ha, o tradir mi vuole.   *Exit.*

[III. xv]

Ghost [*of* ANDREA] *and* REVENGE.

Andrea. Awake, Erichtho! Cerberus, awake!
Solicit Pluto, gentle Proserpine;
To combat, Acheron and Erebus!
For ne'er by Styx and Phlegethon in hell
.   .   .   .   5
Nor ferried Charon to the fiery lakes
Such fearful sights as poor Andrea sees!
Revenge, awake!

---

164. *What else?*] i.e. But of course.
168–9.] He who shows unaccustomed fondness for me has betrayed me or
wants to betray me (Italian).

III.xv.1. *Erichtho*] a Thessalian sorceress (not one of the Furies, as Andrea
seems to think).
3–4. *Acheron, Styx, Phlegethon*] three of the rivers of Hades.
3. *Erebus*] primeval darkness; often the name for hell.
5.] A line appears to be missing here, possibly saying something like *Was
I distressed with outrage sore as this.*

Revenge. Awake? Forwhy?

Andrea. Awake, Revenge, for thou art ill-advised   10
    To sleep; awake! What, thou art warned to watch!

Revenge. Content thyself, and do not trouble me.

Andrea. Awake, Revenge, if love, as love hath had,
    Have yet the power or prevalence in hell!
    Hieronimo with Lorenzo is joined in league   15
    And intercepts our passage to revenge.
    Awake, Revenge, or we are woe-begone!

Revenge. Thus worldlings ground, what they have dreamed,
    upon.
    Content thyself, Andrea; though I sleep,
    Yet is my mood soliciting their souls.   20
    Sufficeth thee that poor Hieronimo
    Cannot forget his son Horatio.
    Nor dies Revenge, although he sleep awhile,
    For in unquiet, quietness is feigned,
    And slumb'ring is a common worldly wile.   25
    Behold, Andrea, for an instance how
    Revenge hath slept, and then imagine thou
    What 'tis to be subject to destiny.

Enter a Dumb Show.

Andrea. Awake, Revenge, reveal this mystery.

Revenge. The two first, the nuptial torches bore,   30
    As brightly burning as the mid-day's sun;
    But after them doth Hymen hie as fast,
    Clothed in sable, and a saffron robe,
    And blows them out and quencheth them with blood,

---

9. *Forwhy?*] Why?

11. *thou . . . watch*] now is a time to be on guard and alert.

13. *love*] i.e. allegiance to my cause.

15.] Hieronimo's mad disguise, intended to avert suspicion by Castile and his family, has fooled Andrea.

18. *ground . . . upon*] found their beliefs on what is a mere dream or fancy.

20.] yet is the spirit of revenge disquieting and importuning their souls.

23-4.] Beneath the agitated surface of events, Revenge is biding its time.

32. *Hymen*] god of marriage, here ominously dressed in *sable* or black (l. 33), though *saffron* (orange-yellow) is more appropriate to nuptials. The Dumb Show presumably takes place as described.

    hie] hasten.

As discontent that things continue so. 35
Andrea. Sufficeth me, thy meaning's understood,
And thanks to thee and those infernal powers
That will not tolerate a lover's woe.
Rest thee, for I will sit to see the rest.
Revenge. Then argue not, for thou hast thy request. 40

Act IV

[IV. i]

Enter BEL-IMPERIA *and* HIERONIMO.

Bel-imperia. Is this the love thou bear'st Horatio?
　　　Is this the kindness that thou counterfeits?
　　　Are these the fruits of thine incessant tears?
　　　Hieronimo, are these thy passions,
　　　Thy protestations and thy deep laments,　　　　　　　5
　　　That thou wert wont to weary men withal?
　　　O unkind father, O deceitful world!
　　　With what excuses canst thou show thyself,
　　　With what　·　·　·　·　·　·
　　　From this dishonour and the hate of men?—　　　　　10
　　　Thus to neglect the loss and life of him
　　　Whom both my letters and thine own belief
　　　Assures thee to be causeless slaughterèd.
　　　Hieronimo, for shame, Hieronimo,
　　　Be not a history to after-times　　　　　　　　　　　15
　　　Of such ingratitude unto thy son.
　　　Unhappy mothers of such children then,
　　　But monstrous fathers, to forget so soon
　　　The death of those whom they with care and cost
　　　Have tendered so, thus careless should be lost.　　　20
　　　Myself, a stranger in respect of thee,
　　　So loved his life as still I wish their deaths,
　　　Nor shall his death be unrevenged by me,

　　IV.i.9.] A part of this line appears to be missing. The whole line may
possibly have read *With what devices seek thyself to save*, or something of the
sort.
　　15. *history*] example, tale.
　　20. *tendered*] cherished, looked after.
　　21.] I, who am a mere stranger to Horatio in comparison with your close
blood ties.
　　22. *still*] constantly.

Although I bear it out for fashion's sake.
For here I swear in sight of heaven and earth,   25
Shouldst thou neglect the love thou shouldst retain
And give it over and devise no more,
Myself should send their hateful souls to hell,
That wrought his downfall with extremest death.

Hieronimo. But may it be that Bel-imperia   30
Vows such revenge as she hath deigned to say?
Why then, I see that heaven applies our drift,
And all the saints do sit soliciting
For vengeance on those cursèd murderers.
Madam, 'tis true, and now I find it so,   35
I found a letter, written in your name,
And in that letter, how Horatio died.
Pardon, O pardon, Bel-imperia,
My fear and care in not believing it,
Nor think I thoughtless think upon a mean   40
To let his death be unrevenged at full;
And here I vow (so you but give consent,
And will conceal my resolution)
I will ere long determine of their deaths,
That causeless thus have murderèd my son.   45

Bel-imperia. Hieronimo, I will consent, conceal,
And aught that may effect for thine avail,
Join with thee to revenge Horatio's death.

Hieronimo. On, then. Whatsoever I devise,
Let me entreat you grace my practices;   50
For why, the plot's already in mine head.
Here they are.

                    Enter BALTHAZAR *and* LORENZO.

Balthazar.   How now, Hieronimo?

24.] although I make a pretence of accepting the situation for the sake of appearances.
32. *applies our drift*] is assisting us towards our goal. *Drift* means 'intent'.
39. *care*] caution.
40.] and do not imagine me so unconcerned as not to think upon a means.
42. *so*] provided that.
44. *determine of*] bring about.
47.] and in anything that may assist you.
50. *grace*] support.

What, courting Bel-imperia?

Hieronimo.   Ay, my lord,
Such courting as, I promise you,
She hath my heart; but you, my lord, have hers.   55

Lorenzo. But now, Hieronimo, or never,
We are to entreat your help.

Hieronimo.   My help?
Why, my good lords, assure yourselves of me,
For you have given me cause,
Ay, by my faith have you.

Balthazar.   It pleased you   60
At the entertainment of the ambassador
To grace the King so much as with a show.
Now, were your study so well furnishèd
As for the passing of the first night's sport
To entertain my father with the like,   65
Or any such-like pleasing motion,
Assure yourself it would content them well.

Hieronimo. Is this all?

Balthazar. Ay, this is all.

Hieronimo. Why then I'll fit you; say no more: 70
When I was young, I gave my mind
And plied myself to fruitless poetry;
Which, though it profit the professor naught,
Yet is it passing pleasing to the world.

Lorenzo. And how for that?

Hieronimo.   Marry, my good lord, thus—   75

62–5.] To be so gracious as to honour the King with a masque. (See
I.iv.137–73.) Now, if your well-furnished learning were able to provide
similar entertainment before my father on the first night's revels celebrating
the wedding . . .

66. *motion*] entertainment, 'show'.

70. *I'll fit you*] (*a*) I'll provide what you need; (*b*) I'll pay you out, I'll
punish you as you deserve. (The second meaning is of course intended for
the audience, not Lorenzo.)

72. *fruitless*] a commonplace characterization of poetry, especially love
poetry.

73. *professor*] practitioner, poet. (Love poetry seldom wins the lady or
makes the poet rich.)

74. *passing*] very.

75. *And how for that?*] and how does this apply?

And yet methinks you are too quick with us—
When in Toledo there I studièd,
It was my chance to write a tragedy,
See here, my lords,   *He shows them a book.*
Which, long forgot, I found this other day.   80
Now would your lordships favour me so much
As but to grace me with your acting it—
I mean each one of you to play a part—
Assure you it will prove most passing strange
And wondrous plausible to that assembly.   85
Balthazar. What, would you have us play a tragedy?
Hieronimo. Why, Nero thought it no disparagement,
    And kings and emperors have ta'en delight
    To make experience of their wits in plays.
Lorenzo. Nay, be not angry, good Hieronimo,   90
    The prince but asked a question.
Balthazar. In faith, Hieronimo, an you be in earnest,
    I'll make one.
Lorenzo. And I another.
Hieronimo. Now, my good lord, could you entreat   95
    Your sister Bel-imperia to make one—
    For what's a play without a woman in it?
Bel-imperia. Little entreaty shall serve me, Hieronimo,
    For I must needs be employed in your play.
Hieronimo. Why, this is well. I tell you, lordings,   100
    It was determinèd to have been acted
    By gentlemen and scholars too,
    Such as could tell what to speak.
Balthazar. And now it shall be played by princes and
        courtiers,

---

77. *there*] there where.
84. *most passing strange*] sensational.
85. *plausible*] acceptable, agreeable, deserving of applause.
87.] Nero's taking part in dramatic contests while emperor of Rome (A.D. 54–68) was considered scandalous by many, and contributed to his unpopularity. Hardly an inspiring model in any case.
89. *experience*] trial.
92. *an*] if.
93. *make one*] take a part.
101. *determinèd*] intended, arranged.
103. *could tell*] knew.

Such as can tell how to speak,   105
    If, as it is our country manner,
    You will but let us know the argument.
Hieronimo. That shall I roundly. The chronicles of Spain
    Record this written of a knight of Rhodes:
    He was betrothed and wedded at the length   110
    To one Perseda, an Italian dame,
    Whose beauty ravished all that her beheld,
    Especially the soul of Soliman,
    Who at the marriage was the chiefest guest.
    By sundry means sought Soliman to win   115
    Perseda's love, and could not gain the same.
    Then gan he break his passions to a friend,
    One of his bashaws whom he held full dear;
    Her had this bashaw long solicited,
    And saw she was not otherwise to be won   120
    But by her husband's death, this knight of Rhodes,
    Whom presently by treachery he slew.
    She, stirred with an exceeding hate therefore,
    As cause of this slew Soliman,
    And to escape the bashaw's tyranny   125
    Did stab herself; and this the tragedy.
Lorenzo. O, excellent!
Bel-imperia.   But say, Hieronimo,
    What then became of him that was the bashaw?
Hieronimo. Marry, thus: moved with remorse of his misdeeds,
    Ran to a mountain top and hung himself.   130
Balthazar. But which of us is to perform that part?
Hieronimo. Oh, that will I, my lords, make no doubt of it;
    I'll play the murderer, I warrant you,
    For I already have conceited that.
Balthazar. And what shall I?   135

---

107. *argument*] plot.
108. *roundly*] directly, without ado.
108-26] Kyd may have written a tragedy, *c.* 1589–1592, about Soliman (i.e. Suleiman, or emperor of the Turks) and Perseda, the beloved and then the wife of Erastus, a knight of Rhodes.
117. *break his passions*] reveal his passion.
118. *bashaws*] pashas, grandees of Turkey.
124. *As cause*] because.
134. *conceited*] formed a conception of.

Hieronimo. Great Soliman, the Turkish emperor.

Lorenzo. And I?

Hieronimo. Erastus, the knight of Rhodes.

Bel-imperia. And I?

Hieronimo. Perseda, chaste and resolute.　　　　　　　140

　And here, my lords, are several abstracts drawn,

　For each of you to note your parts

　And act it as occasion's offered you.

　You must provide a Turkish cap,

　A black mustachio, and a fauchion;　　　　　　　145

　　　　　　　　Gives a paper to BALTHAZAR.

　You with a cross like to a knight of Rhodes;

　　　　　　　　Gives another to LORENZO.

　And madam, you must attire yourself

　　　　　　　　He giveth BEL-IMPERIA *another.*

　Like Phoebe, Flora, or the Huntress,

　Which to your discretion shall seem best.

　And as for me, my lords, I'll look to one,　　　　　　　150

　And with the ransom that the viceroy sent

　So furnish and perform this tragedy

　As all the world shall say Hieronimo

　Was liberal in gracing of it so.

Balthazar. Hieronimo, methinks a comedy were better.　　　155

Hieronimo. A comedy?

　Fie, comedies are fit for common wits;

　But to present a kingly troop withal,

　Give me a stately-written tragedy,

　Tragedia cothurnata, fitting kings,　　　　　　　160

---

141. *several abstracts drawn*] the individual parts separately copied.

142. *note*] i.e. learn.

145. *fauchion*] falchion, a broad curved sword appropriate to the Turkish suleiman.

148.] like Phoebe (associated with the moon), Flora (goddess of fertility and flowers, as at II.iv.25), or Diana (Artemis, goddess of the hunt and of childbirth, also associated with the moon).

150. *look to one*] prepare my role.

152. *furnish and perform*] outfit and produce.

154.] was munificent in lending such graceful adornment to this tragedy.

158.] but to present before a royal audience.

160. *Tragedia cothurnata*] tragedy with actors wearing the buskin or cothurnus, a thick-soled boot reaching to mid leg, as in ancient Greece; hence, the most serious and stately.

Containing matter, and not common things.
My lords, all this must be performed
As fitting for the first night's revelling.
The Italian tragedians were so sharp of wit
That in one hour's meditation   165
They would perform anything in action.
Lorenzo. And well it may, for I have seen the like
    In Paris, 'mongst the French tragedians.
Hieronimo. In Paris? Mass, and well remembered!
    There's one thing more that rests for us to do.   170
Balthazar. What's that, Hieronimo? Forget not anything.
Hieronimo. Each one of us must act his part
    In unknown languages,
    That it may breed the more variety,
    As you, my lord, in Latin, I in Greek,   175
    You in Italian; and for because I know
    That Bel-imperia hath practisèd the French,
    In courtly French shall all her phrases be.
Bel-imperia. You mean to try my cunning then, Hieronimo.
Balthazar. But this will be a mere confusion,   180
    And hardly shall we all be understood.
Hieronimo. It must be so, for the conclusion
    Shall prove the invention and all was good;
    And I myself, in an oration,
    And with a strange and wondrous show besides,   185
    That I will have there behind a curtain,
    Assure yourself, shall make the matter known.
    And all shall be concluded in one scene,
    For there's no pleasure ta'en in tediousness.

---

161. *matter*] i.e. a subject of tragic import.
167. *may*] may be so.
169. *Mass*] by the mass (an oath).
170. *rests*] remains.
176. *for because*] because.
183.] shall prove the worth of the fable and that the whole was a successful tragedy.
187. *shall . . . known*] i.e. will, as epilogue, expound the play (but with a more ominous suggestion, to the audience's ears, of revealing the criminal secrets of Lorenzo).

Balthazar. [*Aside to* LORENZO] How like you this?   190
Lorenzo. [*Aside to* BALTHAZAR] Why thus, my lord:
  We must resolve to soothe his humours up.
Balthazar. On, then, Hieronimo. Farewell till soon.
Hieronimo. You'll ply this gear?
Lorenzo.   I warrant you.
                    Exeunt all but HIERONIMO.
Hieronimo.   Why, so.
  Now shall I see the fall of Babylon,   195
  Wrought by the heavens in this confusion.
  And if the world like not this tragedy,
  Hard is the hap of old Hieronimo.   *Exit.*

[IV. ii]

         Enter ISABELLA *with a weapon.*

Isabella. Tell me no more! O monstrous homicides!
  Since neither piety nor pity moves
  The King to justice or compassion,
  I will revenge myself upon this place
  Where thus they murdered my belovèd son.   5
              She cuts down the arbour.
  Down with these branches and these loathsome boughs
  Of this unfortunate and fatal pine!
  Down with them, Isabella, rend them up
  And burn the roots from whence the rest is sprung!
  I will not leave a root, a stalk, a tree,   10
  A bough, a branch, a blossom, nor a leaf,
  No, not an herb within this garden plot—

192. *soothe his humours up*] humour him.
194. *ply this gear*] work away at this business.
195. *the fall of Babylon*] Revelation xviii is only one of many biblical texts
(see Isaiah xiii–xiv and xxi, Jeremiah l–li, etc.) to invoke the fall of Babylon
as a fulfilment of prophecy and an apocalyptic sign of approaching Last
Judgement. The name also suggests the Tower of Babel (Genesis xi), and
indeed the two were widely confused; the English Bibles of the Renaissance
call Babel 'Babylon' except in Genesis x and xi.

IV.ii.] Location is the garden of Hieronimo's house. The arbour, a stage
property, must be brought onstage again, as in II.iv.

Accursèd complot of my misery.
Fruitless for ever may this garden be,
Barren the earth, and blissless whosoever   15
Imagines not to keep it unmanured!
An eastern wind commixed with noisome airs
Shall blast the plants and the young saplings,
The earth with serpents shall be pesterèd,
And passengers, for fear to be infect,   20
Shall stand aloof, and looking at it, tell,
'There, murdered, died the son of Isabel.'
Ay, here he died, and here I him embrace.
See where his ghost solicits with his wounds
Revenge on her that should revenge his death!   25
Hieronimo, make haste to see thy son,
For sorrow and despair hath cited me
To hear Horatio plead with Rhadamanth.
Make haste, Hieronimo, to hold excused
Thy negligence in pursuit of their deaths,   30
Whose hateful wrath bereaved him of his breath.
Ah, nay, thou dost delay their deaths,
Forgives the murderers of thy noble son,
And none but I bestir me—to no end.
And as I curse this tree from further fruit,   35
So shall my womb be cursèd for his sake,
And with this weapon will I wound the breast,
                                        She stabs herself.
The hapless breast, that gave Horatio suck.   [*Exit.*]

---

13. *complot of*] conspiracy aimed to achieve (with a bitter pun on *plot*, plot of land, in l. 12).

16.] is so dull of perception as not to keep it uncultivated. (Any person of feeling will understand that this cursed piece of land is not to be used henceforth.)

17. *noisome*] noxious. Night air, and certain winds, were thought to be injurious to health.

20. *passengers*] passers-by.

27. *cited*] summoned.

28. *Rhadamanth*] See I.i.33, III.xiii.156, and notes.

29. *hold excused*] make excuses for.

33. *Forgives*] forgivest.

38.S.D. Exit.] Presumably the dying Isabella staggers offstage; her body cannot be visible during the ensuing scene.

[IV. iii]

> *Enter* HIERONIMO; *he knocks up the curtain.*
> *Enter the* DUKE *of* CASTILE.

Castile. How now, Hieronimo, where's your fellows,
  That you take all this pain?
Hieronimo. O sir, it is for the author's credit
  To look that all things may go well.
  But good my lord, let me entreat your grace   5
  To give the King the copy of the play.
  This is the argument of what we show. [*Gives a paper.*]
Castile. I will, Hieronimo.
Hieronimo. One thing more, my good lord.
Castile. What's that?   10
Hieronimo. Let me entreat your grace
  That when the train are passed into the gallery
  You would vouchsafe to throw me down the key.
Castile. I will, Hieronimo.   *Exit* CASTILE.
Hieronimo. What, are you ready, Balthazar?   15
  Bring a chair and a cushion for the King.

> *Enter* BALTHAZAR *with a chair.*

Well done, Balthazar. Hang up the title;

IV.iii.0.1. knocks up the curtain] i.e. fastens up a curtain in a prepared
place, perhaps at a door, in anticipation of a chilling 'discovery' at the
conclusion of 'Soliman and Perseda', IV.iv.88.1.
  6. *the copy of the play*] i.e. the 'book' of the play, such as would be used by
the 'book-keeper' (V.iv.9–10) or prompter—probably not a full script but a
so-called 'plot' (as it is called at IV.iv.33), indicating, scene by scene, actor
assignments, entrances, and important stage business. It is referred to as the
'argument' in the next line (see note) and at IV.iv.10.
  7. *argument*] plot, as at IV.i.107.
  12.] that when the King and his retinue have proceeded into the hall.
(They will see the play from the main stage, where the King's chair is set at
l. 16.1, not from the upper gallery.)
  13. *throw ... key*] i.e. throw the key down on the floor for me. (See
previous note.) Hieronimo asks for the key ostensibly so that he can proceed
with arrangements for the play, evidently in the Duke of Castile's house; but
see IV.iv.156 and n. for his ulterior motive.
  17. *Hang up the title*] suggesting that in this play, as in some others, title-
boards could be used onstage to indicate locality of some scenes (though not
for the more fluid sense of place that is so common in Elizabethan scripts).

Our scene is Rhodes. What, is your beard on?
Balthazar. Half on, the other is in my hand.
Hieronimo. Dispatch, for shame; are you so long? 20

Exit BALTHAZAR.

Bethink thyself, Hieronimo.
Recall thy wits, recount thy former wrongs
Thou hast received by murder of thy son,
And lastly, not least, how Isabel,
Once his mother and thy dearest wife, 25
All woe-begone for him, hath slain herself.
Behoves thee then, Hieronimo, to be revenged!
The plot is laid of dire revenge.
On then, Hieronimo, pursue revenge,
For nothing wants but acting of revenge.

Exit HIERONIMO.

[IV. iv]

Enter Spanish KING, VICEROY, *the* DUKE *of* CASTILE,
and their train.

King. Now, Viceroy, shall we see the tragedy
Of Soliman the Turkish emperor,
Performed of pleasure by your son the prince,
My nephew, Don Lorenzo, and my niece.
Viceroy. Who, Bel-imperia? 5
King. Ay, and Hieronimo our marshal,
At whose request they deign to do't themselves.
These be our pastimes in the court of Spain.
Here brother, you shall be the book-keeper:
This is the argument of that they show. 10

He giveth him a book.

---

22. *recount*] call to memory.

IV.iv.] The scene essentially continues from IV.iii, with the King's chair
placed for him to watch Hieronimo's tragedy, and the curtain hung up for
the 'discovery' effect at l. 88.1; but the stage is cleared of actors for a moment,
and editors conventionally mark a new scene.

3. *of pleasure*] Prince Balthazar and the rest are graciously pleased to
consent to be actors in the tragedy. On the propriety of aristocrats being
actors, compare l. 7 below and IV.i.86–104.

10.1. a book] probably not a full script, but a stage 'plot'; see IV.iii.6–7
and notes and l. 33 below.

Gentlemen, this play of HIERONIMO *in sundry languages was
thought good to be set down in English more largely,
for the easier understanding to every public reader.*

Enter BALTHAZAR, BEL-IMPERIA, *and* HIERONIMO.

*Balthazar. Bashaw, that Rhodes is ours, yield heavens the
      honour,
   And holy Mahomet, our sacred prophet;
   And be thou graced with every excellence
   That Soliman can give, or thou desire.
   But thy desert in conquering Rhodes is less   15
   Than in reserving this fair Christian nymph,
   Perseda, blissful lamp of excellence,
   Whose eyes compel, like powerful adamant,
   The warlike heart of Soliman to wait.*
King. See, Viceroy, that is Balthazar your son   20
   That represents the emperor Soliman.
   How well he acts his amorous passion!
Viceroy. Ay, Bel-imperia hath taught him that.
Castile. That's because his mind runs all on Bel-imperia.
Hieronimo. Whatever joy earth yields betide your majesty.   25
Balthazar. Earth yields no joy without Perseda's love.
Hieronimo. Let then Perseda on your grace attend.
*Balthazar. She shall not wait on me; but I on her.
   Drawn by the influence of her lights, I yield.
   But let my friend, the Rhodian knight, come forth,   30
   Erasto, dearer than my life to me,
   That he may see Perseda, my beloved.*

10.2–4.] This note to gentlemen readers maintains the fiction that the
actors perform in different languages, as Hieronimo has warned his actors at
IV.i.172–8 and as he reiterates at l. 74 in the present scene, but presumably
the original performances were in English throughout. Audiences readily
accept the convention that they are 'hearing' other languages.

   10.3. more largely] in full, throughout.
   16. reserving] sparing the life of and setting apart for special use.
   18. adamant] a magnet.
   19. to wait] to attend on her.
   25. Hieronimo] Hieronimo plays the Bashaw, villainous counsellor to the
emperor Soliman.
   29. the . . . lights] the powerful force emanating from her eyes, like the
influence that was thought to stream from the heavenly bodies in an ethereal
fluid acting upon the character and destiny of humans.

Enter Erasto.

King. Here comes Lorenzo; look upon the plot,
  And tell me, brother, what part plays he?
Bel-imperia. *Ah, my Erasto, welcome to Perseda.*   35
Lorenzo. *Thrice happy is Erasto that thou liv'st.*
  Rhodes' loss is nothing to Erasto's joy;
  Sith his Perseda lives, his life survives.
                    [*Soliman confers aside with his Bashaw.*]
Balthazar. *Ah, Bashaw, here is love between Erasto*
  And fair Perseda, sovereign of my soul.   40
Hieronimo. *Remove Erasto, mighty Soliman,*
  And then Perseda will be quickly won.
Balthazar. *Erasto is my friend, and while he lives*
  Perseda never will remove her love.
Hieronimo. *Let not Erasto live to grieve great Soliman.*   45
Balthazar. *Dear is Erasto in our princely eye.*
Hieronimo. *But if he be your rival, let him die.*
Balthazar. *Why, let him die; so love commandeth me.*
  Yet grieve I that Erasto should so die.
                    [*The Bashaw approaches Erasto.*]
Hieronimo. *Erasto, Soliman saluteth thee,*   50
  And lets thee wit by me his highness' will,
  Which is, thou shouldst be thus employed.   Stab him.
Bel-imperia.   Ay me,
  Erasto! See, Soliman, Erasto's slain!
Balthazar. *Yet liveth Soliman to comfort thee.*
  Fair queen of beauty, let not favour die,   55
  But with a gracious eye behold his grief
  That with Perseda's beauty is increased,
  If by Perseda grief be not released.
Bel-imperia. *Tyrant, desist soliciting vain suits!*

---

33. *the plot*] This theatrical abridgement can tell Castile as 'book-keeper'
(l. 9) how the parts are assigned.
  37. to] compared to.
  51. wit] know.
  55. favour] liking, good will. Soliman begs Perseda to bestow her love on
him.
  56–8.] but graciously behold the grief of him (i.e. myself) whose grief will
only be accentuated by Perseda's (i.e. your) beauty unless she (you) release
him (me) from his (my) grief (by granting his (my) love suit).

Relentless are mine ears to thy laments   60
As thy butcher is pitiless and base
Which seized on my Erasto, harmless knight.
Yet by thy power thou thinkest to command,
And to thy power Perseda doth obey.
But were she able, thus she would revenge   65
Thy treacheries on thee, ignoble prince;   *Stab him.*
And on herself she would be thus revenged.   *Stab herself.*

King. Well said, old Marshal, this was bravely done!
Hieronimo. But Bel-imperia plays Perseda well.
Viceroy. Were this in earnest, Bel-imperia,   70
      You would be better to my son than so.
King. But now what follows for Hieronimo?
Hieronimo. Marry, this follows for Hieronimo:
      Here break we off our sundry languages,
      And thus conclude I in our vulgar tongue.   75
      Haply you think, but bootless are your thoughts,
      That this is fabulously counterfeit,
      And that we do as all tragedians do:
      To die today, for fashioning our scene,
      The death of Ajax, or some Roman peer,   80
      And in a minute starting up again
      Revive to please tomorrow's audience.
      No, princes, know I am Hieronimo,
      The hopeless father of a hapless son,
      Whose tongue is tuned to tell his latest tale,   85
      Not to excuse gross errors in the play.
      I see your looks urge instance of these words.
      Behold the reason urging me to this.
                              Shows his dead son.

---

60. Relentless] as unyielding.
61. thy butcher] the Bashaw.
68.] Well done, Hieronimo, excellently done!
75. *vulgar*] vernacular.
76. *bootless*] unavailing.
77. *fabulously*] fictitiously, in a mere fable.
85–6.] I whose tongue is ready to tell the end of Horatio's story, not, like a usual epilogue, apologize for the play.
87. *instance*] evidence, a concrete example.
88.1.] Hieronimo draws back the curtain he hung up at IV.iii.0.1, presumably over a stage door; the body of Horatio has meantime been readied for this shocking 'discovery'.

See here my show, look on this spectacle:
Here lay my hope, and here my hope hath end;   90
Here lay my heart, and here my heart was slain;
Here lay my treasure, here my treasure lost;
Here lay my bliss, and here my bliss bereft;
But hope, heart, treasure, joy and bliss,
All fled, failed, died, yea, all decayed with this.   95
From forth these wounds came breath that gave me life;
They murdered me that made these fatal marks.
The cause was love, whence grew this mortal hate,
The hate, Lorenzo and young Balthazar,
The love, my son to Bel-imperia.   100
But night, the coverer of accursèd crimes,
With pitchy silence hushed these traitors' harms
And lent them leave, for they had sorted leisure
To take advantage in my garden plot
Upon my son, my dear Horatio.   105
There, merciless, they butchered up my boy,
In black dark night, to pale dim cruel death.
He shrieks! I heard, and yet methinks I hear,
His dismal outcry echo in the air.
With soonest speed I hasted to the noise,   110
Where, hanging on a tree, I found my son,
Through-girt with wounds, and slaughtered as you see.
And grieved I, think you, at this spectacle?
Speak, Portuguese, whose loss resembles mine:
If thou canst weep upon thy Balthazar,   115
'Tis like I wailed for my Horatio.
And you, my lord, whose reconcilèd son
Marched in a net, and thought himself unseen,

102–3. *With . . . leave*] with pitch-darkness muffled the sounds of the
malicious deeds of these traitors and permitted them to act.
103. *sorted leisure*] sought out an opportunity.
108. *methinks I hear*] it seems to me that I hear still.
112. *Through-girt*] pierced.
116. *'Tis like*] it is likely that, it follows as a logical necessity.
117. *you*] the Duke of Castile.
reconcilèd] Hieronimo seems to refer ironically to his pretended reconcili-
ation with Lorenzo at III.xiv.130–64.
118.] acted deceitfully and clandestinely, supposing himself able to avoid
detection.

And rated me for brainsick lunacy,
With 'God amend that mad Hieronimo!'—   120
How can you brook our play's catastrophe?
And here behold this bloody handkerchief,
Which at Horatio's death I weeping dipped
Within the river of his bleeding wounds;
It as propitious, see, I have reserved,   125
And never hath it left my bloody heart,
Soliciting remembrance of my vow
With these, O these accursèd murderers,
Which, now performed, my heart is satisfied.
And to this end the bashaw I became   130
That might revenge me on Lorenzo's life,
Who therefore was appointed to the part
And was to represent the knight of Rhodes,
That I might kill him more conveniently.
So, Viceroy, was this Balthazar, thy son,   135
That Soliman which Bel-imperia
In person of Perseda murderèd,
Solely appointed to that tragic part
That she might slay him that offended her.
Poor Bel-imperia missed her part in this,   140
For, though the story saith she should have died,
Yet I of kindness and of care to her
Did otherwise determine of her end;
But love of him whom they did hate too much
Did urge her resolution to be such.   145
And princes, now behold Hieronimo,
Author and actor in this tragedy,
Bearing his latest fortune in his fist;
And will as resolute conclude his part

---

119. *rated*] berated.
121. *brook*] tolerate.
125.] see, I have kept it constantly with me as an omen and a reminder.
128. *With these*] i.e. to be even with these.
140. *missed her part*] Hieronimo explains how he rewrote the story so that
Bel-imperia (in the role of Perseda) would not have to die, as the tragedy
originally dictated; but she, for love of Horatio 'whom they [Lorenzo and
Balthazar] did hate too much' (l. 144), insisted on carrying through with the
death of Perseda and hence of herself.

As any of the actors gone before.   150
And gentles, thus I end my play.
Urge no more words, I have no more to say.
                                    He runs to hang himself.
King. O, hearken, Viceroy! Hold, Hieronimo!
Brother, my nephew and thy son are slain!
Viceroy. We are betrayed! My Balthazar is slain!   155
Break ope the doors, run, save Hieronimo!
                    [*They break in, and hold* HIERONIMO.]
Hieronimo, do but inform the King of these events;
Upon mine honour thou shalt have no harm.
Hieronimo. Viceroy, I will not trust thee with my life,
Which I this day have offered to my son.   160
Accursèd wretch,
Why stayest thou him that was resolved to die?
King. Speak, traitor; damnèd bloody murderer, speak!
For now I have thee I will make thee speak.
Why hast thou done this undeserving deed?   165
Viceroy. Why hast thou murderèd my Balthazar?
Castile. Why hast thou butchered both my children thus?
Hieronimo. O, good words!   [*Fifth Addition; see pp. 141–3*]
As dear to me was my Horatio
As yours, or yours, or yours, my lord, to you.   170
My guiltless son was by Lorenzo slain,
And by Lorenzo and that Balthazar
Am I at last revengèd thoroughly,

152.1.] This stage direction, and the action of breaking open he doors at l. 156, suggest the use of a specially defined stage area for the attempted hanging. Perhaps, with thematic fitness, the trellis or arbour used to hang Horatio in II.iv, and possibly too to hang Pedringano in III.vi, is pressed into service once more.

156.] Castile has done as Hieronimo asked at IV.iii.12–13 (see notes there), and so only Hieronimo has the key to the hall where they are now locked in.

156.1.] This stage direction is from the edition of 1602, and relates to a revival of *The Spanish Tragedy* a decade or more after it was first produced, but the action seems necessary. Perhaps attendants or guards 'break in' from offstage and hold Hieronimo, who is certainly guarded while the King addresses him.

161. *Accursèd wretch*] probably addressed to one of the attendants restraining Hieronimo.

172. *by*] by the deaths of.

Upon whose souls may heavens be yet avenged
With greater far than these afflictions.   175
Castile. But who were thy confederates in this?
Viceroy. That was thy daughter Bel-imperia,
    For by her hand my Balthazar was slain.
    I saw her stab him.
King.   Why speak'st thou not?
Hieronimo. What lesser liberty can kings afford   180
    Than harmless silence? Then afford it me.
    Sufficeth I may not, nor I will not tell thee.
King. Fetch forth the tortures.
    Traitor as thou art, I'll make thee tell.
Hieronimo.   Indeed,
    Thou may'st torment me, as his wretched son   185
    Hath done in murdering my Horatio,
    But never shalt thou force me to reveal
    The thing which I have vowed inviolate;
    And therefore, in despite of all thy threats,
    Pleased with their deaths, and eased with their revenge,   190
    First take my tongue, and afterwards my heart.
                                    [*He bites out his tongue.*]
King. O, monstrous resolution of a wretch!
    See, Viceroy, he hath bitten forth his tongue
    Rather than to reveal what we required.
Castile. Yet can he write.   195
King. And if in this he satisfy us not,
    We will devise th'extremest kind of death
    That ever was invented for a wretch.
                Then he makes signs for a knife to mend his pen.
Castile. Oh, he would have a knife to mend his pen.
Viceroy. Here, and advise thee that thou write the truth.   200
King. Look to my brother! Save Hieronimo.
                He with a knife stabs the DUKE *and himself.*
    What age hath ever heard such monstrous deeds?
    My brother, and the whole succeeding hope
    That Spain expected after my decease!
    Go bear his body hence, that we may mourn   205
    The loss of our belovèd brother's death,

---

200. *advise thee*] see to it, take care.

That he may be entombed whate'er befall.
I am the next, the nearest, last of all.
Viceroy. And thou, Don Pedro, do the like for us;
Take up our hapless son, untimely slain. 210
Set me with him, and he with woeful me,
Upon the mainmast of a ship unmanned,
And let the wind and tide haul me along
To Scylla's barking and untamèd gulf,
Or to the loathsome pool of Acheron, 215
To weep my want for my sweet Balthazar.
Spain hath no refuge for a Portingale.

The trumpets sound a dead march, the KING *of* Spain *mourning after his brother's body, and the* KING *of* Portingale *bearing the body of his son.*

[IV. v]

Ghost [*of* ANDREA] *and* REVENGE.

Andrea. Ay, now my hopes have end in their effects,
When blood and sorrow finish my desires:
Horatio murdered in his father's bower,
Vile Serberine by Pedringano slain,
False Pedringano hanged by quaint device, 5
Fair Isabella by herself misdone,
Prince Balthazar by Bel-imperia stabbed,
The Duke of Castile and his wicked son
Both done to death by old Hieronimo,
My Bel-imperia fall'n as Dido fell, 10
And good Hieronimo slain by himself—
Ay, these were spectacles to please my soul.
Now will I beg at lovely Proserpine,
That by the virtue of her princely doom

---

214. *Scylla*] a sea monster opposite the whirlpool, Charybdis, in the Straits of Messina (here described as a 'barking and untamèd gulf').
215. *Acheron*] one of the rivers of Hades, as at I.i.19.
216. *my want for*] my loss of.

IV.v.5. *quaint*] ingenious.
6. *misdone*] done in, killed.
10. *as Dido fell*] Dido's suicide after the departure of Aeneas is described in Bk IV of Virgil's *Aeneid*.

I may consort my friends in pleasing sort,   15
And on my foes work just and sharp revenge.
I'll lead my friend Horatio through those fields
Where never-dying wars are still inured;
I'll lead fair Isabella to that train
Where pity weeps but never feeleth pain;   20
I'll lead my Bel-imperia to those joys
That vestal virgins and fair queens possess;
I'll lead Hieronimo where Orpheus plays,
Adding sweet pleasure to eternal days.
But say, Revenge, for thou must help or none,   25
Against the rest how shall my hate be shown?
Revenge. This hand shall hale them down to deepest hell,
Where none but furies, bugs, and tortures dwell.
Andrea. Then, sweet Revenge, do this at my request:
Let me be judge, and doom them to unrest.   30
Let loose poor Tityus from the vulture's gripe,
And let Don Cyprian supply his room;
Place Don Lorenzo on Ixion's wheel,
And let the lover's endless pains surcease
(Juno forgets old wrath and grants him ease);   35
Hang Balthazar about Chimaera's neck,
And let him there bewail his bloody love,
Repining at our joys that are above;
Let Serberine go roll the fatal stone,
And take from Sisyphus his endless moan;   40
False Pedringano, for his treachery,

---

15. *consort*] accompany.
18. *inured*] practised, carried on.
19. *train*] company; way of existence.
28. *bugs*] bugbears, horrifying objects.
31. *Tityus*] a giant who, for offering violence to Leto (the mother of Apollo and Artemis), was condemned to Hades where two vultures tore at his liver.
32. *supply his room*] take his place.
34. *the lover*] Ixion had tried to seduce Hera or Juno; compare I.i.66.
surcease] cease.
36. *Chimaera*] a fire-breathing monster with the head of a lion, the body of a goat and the tail of a dragon.
37. *his bloody love*] Bel-imperia, having stabbed herself.
39. *fatal*] Whenever Sisyphus laboriously rolled his stone to the top of a hill in Hades it rolled back down again, so that his punishment was eternal.

Let him be dragged through boiling Acheron,
And there live, dying still in endless flames,
Blaspheming gods and all their holy names.
Revenge. Then haste we down to meet thy friends and foes,   45
To place thy friends in ease, the rest in woes;
For here though death hath end their misery,
I'll there begin their endless tragedy.   *Exeunt*.

---

47. *end*] ended.

Additional passages from the edition of 1602

FIRST ADDITION

(Between II. v. 45 and 46. See p. 55)

[*Isabella.*] *For outrage fits our cursèd wretchedness.*
    Ay me, Hieronimo, sweet husband, speak!
Hieronimo. He supped with us tonight, frolic and merry,
    And said he would go visit Balthazar
    At the duke's palace; there the prince doth lodge.
    He had no custom to stay out so late;   5
    He may be in his chamber. Some go see.
    Roderigo, ho!

Enter PEDRO *and* JAQUES.

Isabella. Ay me, he raves. Sweet Hieronimo!
Hieronimo. True, all Spain takes note of it.
    Besides, he is so generally beloved,   10
    His majesty the other day did grace him
    With waiting on his cup. These be favours
    Which do assure he cannot be short-lived.
Isabella. Sweet Hieronimo!
Hieronimo. I wonder how this fellow got his clothes.   15
    Sirrah, sirrah, I'll know the truth of all.
    Jaques, run to the Duke of Castile's presently,
    And bid my son Horatio to come home.
    I and his mother have had strange dreams tonight.
    Do ye hear me, sir?
Jaques.   Ay, sir.
Hieronimo.   Well sir, begone.   20
                          [*Exit* JAQUES.]
    Pedro, come hither. Knowest thou who this is?
Pedro. Too well, sir.
Hieronimo. Too well? Who? Who is it? Peace, Isabella.
    Nay, blush not, man.

Pedro. It is my lord Horatio.

Hieronimo. Ha, ha! Saint James, but this doth make me laugh, 25
That there are more deluded than myself.

Pedro. Deluded?

Hieronimo. Ay, I would have sworn myself within this hour
That this had been my son Horatio,
His garments are so like. Ha! 30
Are they not great persuasions?

Isabella. O, would to God it were not so!

Hieronimo. Were not, Isabella? Dost thou dream it is?
Can thy soft bosom entertain a thought
That such a black deed of mischief should be done 35
On one so pure and spotless as our son?
Away, I am ashamèd.

Isabella. Dear Hieronimo,
Cast a more serious eye upon thy grief.
Weak apprehension gives but weak belief.

Hieronimo. It was a man, sure, that was hanged up here, 40
A youth, as I remember; I cut him down.
If it should prove my son now after all—
Say you? Say you? Light! Lend me a taper,
Let me look again. O God!
Confusion, mischief, torment, death and hell, 45
Drop all your stings at once in my cold bosom,
That now is stiff with horror! Kill me quickly.
Be gracious to me, thou infective night,
And drop this deed of murder down on me.
Gird in my waste of grief with thy large darkness, 50
And let me not survive to see the light
May put me in the mind I had a son.

Isabella. O sweet Horatio, O my dearest son!

Hieronimo. How strangely had I lost my way to grief.
Sweet lovely rose, ill-plucked before thy time,

First Addition
26. *more deluded*] others more deluded.
50. *Gird . . . grief*] confine, limit my wasting grief. (*Waste* puns on *waist*; the two words could be spelled the same, and would be indistinguishable in the theatre.)

SECOND ADDITION

(Replacing Hieronimo's speech, III. ii. 65–6. See p. 65)

Lorenzo. Why so, Hieronimo? Use me.
Hieronimo.   Who, you, my lord?
    I reserve your favour for a greater honour.
    This is a very toy, my lord, a toy.
Lorenzo. All's one, Hieronimo, acquaint me with it.
Hieronimo. I'faith, my lord, it is an idle thing,   5
    I must confess; I ha' been too slack, too tardy,
    Too remiss unto your honour.
Lorenzo.   How now, Hieronimo?
Hieronimo. In troth, my lord, it is a thing of nothing,
    The murder of a son, or so;
    A thing of nothing, my lord.   10
Lorenzo.   *Why then, farewell.*

THIRD ADDITION

(Between III. xi. 1 and 2. See p. 89)

First Portuguese. By your leave, sir.
Hieronimo. 'Tis neither as you think, nor as you think,
    Nor as you think; you're wide all.
    These slippers are not mine, they were my son Horatio's.
    My son! And what's a son? A thing begot
    Within a pair of minutes, thereabout;   5
    A lump bred up in darkness, and doth serve
    To ballast these light creatures we call women;
    And at nine moneths' end, creeps forth to light.
    What is there yet in a son
    To make a father dote, rave or run mad?   10

Second Addition

2.] I would rather save your offer of patronage for a more important occasion.

3. *toy*] trifle.

4. *All's one*] that's all right, never mind that.

Third Addition

2. *wide*] wide of the mark.

Being born, it pouts, cries and breeds teeth.
What is there yet in a son? He must be fed,
Be taught to go, and speak. Ay, or yet?
Why might not a man love a calf as well?
Or melt in passion o'er a frisking kid   15
As for a son? Methinks a young bacon
Or a fine little smooth horse-colt
Should move a man as much as doth a son;
For one of these in very little time
Will grow to some good use, whereas a son,   20
The more he grows in stature and in years,
The more unsquared, unbevelled, he appears,
Reckons his parents among the rank of fools,
Strikes care upon their heads with his mad riots,
Makes them look old before they meet with age.   25
This is a son.
And what a loss were this, considered truly?
Oh, but my Horatio
Grew out of reach of these insatiate humours;
He loved his loving parents,   30
He was my comfort and his mother's joy,
The very arm that did hold up our house.
Our hopes were storèd up in him;
None but a damnèd murderer could hate him.
He had not seen the back of nineteen year,   35
When his strong arm unhorsed the proud Prince
    Balthazar,
And his great mind, too full of honour,
Took him unto mercy,
That valiant but ignoble Portingale.
Well, heaven is heaven still,   40
And there is Nemesis and Furies,
And tnings called whips,
And they sometimes do meet with murderers;
They do not always scape, that's some comfort.

---

13. *go*] walk.
Ay, or yet?] i.e. again, what is a son?
16. *bacon*] i.e. pig.
22. *unsquared, unbevelled*] untidy, not cut at neat angles; undisciplined.
24. *riots*] riotous behaviour.

Ay, ay, ay, and then time steal on,   45
And steals, and steals, till violence leaps forth
Like thunder wrappèd in a ball of fire,
And so doth bring confusion to them all.
Good leave have you. Nay, I pray you go,

FOURTH ADDITION

(Between III. xii and III, xiii, with final stage-direction replacing
III. xiii. 0.1. See p. 94)

Enter JAQUES *and* PEDRO [*with torches*].

Jaques. I wonder, Pedro, why our master thus
    At midnight sends us with our torches' light,
    When man and bird and beast are all at rest,
    Save those that watch for rape and bloody murder?
Pedro. O Jaques, know thou that our master's mind   5
    Is much distraught since his Horatio died,
    And, now his agèd years should sleep in rest,
    His heart in quiet, like a desperate man
    Grows lunatic and childish for his son.
    Sometimes, as he doth at his table sit,   10
    He speaks as if Horatio stood by him,
    Then starting in a rage, falls on the earth,
    Cries out, 'Horatio! Where is my Horatio?'
    So that with extreme grief and cutting sorrow
    There is not left in him one inch of man.   15
    See where he comes.

Enter HIERONIMO.

Hieronimo. I pry through every crevice of each wall,
    Look on each tree, and search through every brake,
    Beat at the bushes, stamp our grandam earth,

---

48. *confusion*] destruction.

Fourth Addition
4. *watch*] stay awake and vigilant.
7. *now*] now when.
18. *brake*] thicket.
19. *grandam*] grandmother.

Dive in the water, and stare up to heaven,   20
Yet cannot I behold my son Horatio.
How now? Who's there? Sprites? Sprites?
Pedro. We are your servants that attend you, sir.
Hieronimo. What make you with your torches in the dark?
Pedro. You bid us light them and attend you here.   25
Hieronimo. No, no, you are deceived; not I, you are deceived.
    Was I so mad to bid you light your torches now?
    Light me your torches at the mid of noon,
    Whenas the sun-god rides in all his glory;
    Light me your torches then.
Pedro.   Then we burn daylight.   30
Hieronimo. Let it be burnt. Night is a murderous slut
    That would not have her treasons to be seen,
    And yonder pale-faced Hecate there, the moon,
    Doth give consent to that is done in darkness,
    And all those stars that gaze upon her face   35
    Are aglets on her sleeve, pins on her train;
    And those that should be powerful and divine
    Do sleep in darkness when they most should shine.
Pedro. Provoke them not, fair sir, with tempting words.
    The heavens are gracious, and your miseries   40
    And sorrow makes you speak you know not what.
Hieronimo. Villain, thou liest, and thou doest naught
    But tell me I am mad. Thou liest, I am not mad.
    I know thee to be Pedro, and he Jaques.
    I'll prove it to thee, and, were I mad, how could I?   45
    Where was she that same night when my Horatio
    Was murdered? She should have shone; search thou the
        book.

---

24. *What make you*] what are you doing.

29. *Whenas*] when.

30. *burn daylight*] waste time (a common phrase), with literal application
to the torches.

34. *that*] whatever.

36. *aglets*] metal tags for laces; any metallic stud, plate, or spangle worn on
the dress.

45. *it*] i.e. what I said a moment ago, that the moon and stars 'Do sleep in
darkness when they most should shine' (l. 38).

47. *the book*] the almanac.

Had the moon shone, in my boy's face there was a kind
  of grace
That, I know, nay, I do know, had the murderer seen
  him,
His weapon would have fall'n and cut the earth,   50
Had he been framed of naught but blood and death.
Alack, when mischief doth it knows not what,
What shall we say to mischief?

Enter ISABELLA.

Isabella. Dear Hieronimo, come in a-doors.
  O, seek not means so to increase thy sorrow.   55
Hieronimo. Indeed, Isabella, we do nothing here.
  I do not cry; ask Pedro and ask Jaques.
  Not I indeed; we are very merry, very merry.
Isabella. How? Be merry here, be merry here?
  Is not this the place, and this the very tree,   60
  Where my Horatio died, where he was murdered?
Hieronimo. Was—do not say what; let her weep it out.
  This was the tree; I set it of a kernel,
  And when our hot Spain could not let it grow,
  But that the infant and the human sap   65
  Began to wither, duly twice a morning
  Would I be sprinkling it with fountain water.
  At last it grew, and grew, and bore and bore,
  Till at the length
  It grew a gallows, and did bear our son.   70
  It bore thy fruit and mine. O wicked, wicked plant!

One knocks within at the door.

---

51. *Had he*] even if he had.
framed] made.
52. *mischief*] evil, harm.
60. *the very tree*] The language of this added passage suggests a performance in which Horatio was hanged from a stage tree, one that is onstage again
for this scene, or else is represented by a pillar or such. Compare the stage
direction at II.iv.53.1 indicating that '*They hang him [Horatio] in the arbour*'.
62. *Was—*] Hieronimo is about to ask some question of his men, but
interrupts himself out of concern for Isabella.
71.1. within at the door] from within the tiring house or dressing room
backstage, on the inside of a stage door.

See who knock there.

Pedro.   It is a painter, sir.

Hieronimo. Bid him come in, and paint some comfort,
    For surely there's none lives but painted comfort.
    Let him come in. One knows not what may chance.   75
    God's will, that I should set this tree!—But even so
    Masters ungrateful servants rear from naught,
    And then they hate them that did bring them up.

                    Enter the Painter.

Painter. God bless you, sir.

Hieronimo. Wherefore? Why, thou scornful villain,   80
    How, where, or by what means should I be blessed?

Isabella. What wouldst thou have, good fellow?

Painter. Justice, madam.

Hieronimo. O ambitious beggar, wouldst thou have that
    That lives not in the world?   85
    Why, all the undelved mines cannot buy
    An ounce of justice, 'tis a jewel so inestimable.
    I tell thee,
    God hath engrossed all justice in his hands,
    And there is none but what comes from him.   90

Painter. O, then I see
    That God must right me for my murdered son.

Hieronimo. How, was thy son murdered?

Painter. Ay, sir. No man did hold a son so dear.

Hieronimo. What, not as thine? That's a lie   95
    As massy as the earth. I had a son,
    Whose least unvalued hair did weigh
    A thousand of thy sons; and he was murdered.

Painter. Alas, sir, I had no more but he.

---

72. *knock*] knocks.

73. *paint*] depict, show us. Hieronimo goes on to pun bitterly on the word
in the next line: painted comfort is illusory hope.

76. *God's will, that*] in the name of God, to think that.
even so] in just the same way.

78. *they hate them*] servants hate masters.

80–1.] Hieronimo answers the Painter's conventional greeting as a
serious philosophical assertion. Isabella steps in, seeing that the Painter is
nonplussed.

89. *engrossed*] monopolized.

Hieronimo. Nor, I, nor I; but this same one of mine   100
    Was worth a legion. But all is one.
    Pedro, Jaques, go in a-doors; Isabella, go;
    And this good fellow here and I
    Will range this hideous orchard up and down,
    Like to two lions reavèd of their young.   105
    Go in a-doors, I say.

              Exeunt [ISABELLA, PEDRO, JAQUES].

        The Painter *and he sits down.*

    Come, let's talk wisely now. Was thy son murdered?
Painter. Ay, sir.
Hieronimo. So was mine. How dost take it? Art thou not
    sometimes mad? Is there no tricks that comes before   110
    thine eyes?
Painter. O Lord, yes, sir.
Hieronimo. Art a painter? Canst paint me a tear, or a wound,
    a groan, or a sigh? Canst paint me such a tree as this?
Painter. Sir, I am sure you have heard of my painting. My   115
    name's Bazardo.
Hieronimo. Bazardo! Afore God, an excellent fellow. Look
    you, sir, do you see, I'd have you paint me in my gallery,
    in your oil colours matted, and draw me five years
    younger than I am—do you see, sir, let five years go, let   120
    them go—like the marshal of Spain; my wife Isabella
    standing by me; with a speaking look to my son Horatio,
    which should intend to this or some such like purpose:
    'God bless thee, my sweet son,' and my hand leaning
    upon his head, thus sir, do you see? May it be done?   125
Painter. Very well, sir.
Hieronimo. Nay, I pray mark me, sir. Then, sir, would I have

---

    101. *all is one*] no matter.
    105. *reavèd*] bereaved, forcibly deprived.
    110. *tricks*] illusions.
    119. *matted*] made dull or matt, or, possibly, mounted with a mat.
    122. *a speaking look*] Renaissance artists and theorists were fascinated with
the idea that painting is a speaking picture (ecphrasis). In ll. 139-43, the
Painter is instructed to portray a loud noise and Hieronimo's outcry. See also
ll. 155-61.
    123. *intend to*] signify.

you paint me this tree, this very tree. Canst paint a doleful
cry?

Painter. Seemingly, sir.   130

Hieronimo. Nay, it should cry; but all is one. Well sir, paint
me a youth, run through and through with villains'
swords, hanging upon this tree. Canst thou draw a
murderer?

Painter. I'll warrant you, sir. I have the pattern of the most   135
notorious villains that ever lived in all Spain.

Hieronimo. O, let them be worse, worse. Stretch thine art, and
let their beards be of Judas his own colour, and let their
eyebrows jutty over; in any case observe that. Then, sir,
after some violent noise, bring me forth in my shirt, and   140
my gown under mine arm, with my torch in my hand,
and my sword reared up thus; and with these words:
        What noise is this? Who calls Hieronimo?
May it be done?

Painter. Yea, sir.   145

Hieronimo. Well sir, then bring me forth, bring me through
alley and alley, still with a distracted countenance going
along, and let my hair heave up my night-cap. Let the
clouds scowl, make the moon dark, the stars extinct, the
winds blowing, the bells tolling, the owl shrieking,   150
the toads croaking, the minutes jarring, and the clock
striking twelve. And then at last, sir, starting, behold a
man hanging, and tottering and tottering, as you know
the wind will weave a man, and I with a trice to cut him
down. And looking upon him by the advantage of my   155

---

130. *Seemingly*] realistically.

131. *all is one*] never mind that.

138. *Judas his own colour*] Judas's own colour, red.

139. *jutty*] jut, project.

146-61.] The imagined painting will not only portray speaking gestures,
noise, and outcries (see n. 122 above), but will move through a sequence of
events spread out in time.

147. *alley*] garden-walk.

151. *jarring*] ticking; with suggestion also of a harsh, grating sound.

152. *starting*] The Painter is to show Hieronimo starting with amazement
and horror as he sees the hanging corpse.

153. *tottering*] swinging to and fro at the end of a rope. (The word also
describes Hieronimo staggering in amazement.)

154. *weave*] cause to sway.
with a trice] in a trice.

torch, find it to be my son Horatio. There you may show
a passion, there you may show a passion. Draw me like
old Priam of Troy, crying, 'The house is a-fire, the house
is a-fire, as the torch over my head.' Make me curse,
make me rave, make me cry, make me mad, make me   160
well again, make me curse hell, invocate heaven, and, in
the end, leave me in a trance—and so forth.

Painter. And is this the end?

Hieronimo. O no, there is no end; the end is death and madness. As I am never better than when I am mad, then   165
methinks I am a brave fellow, then I do wonders; but
reason abuseth me, and there's the torment, there's the
hell. At the last, sir, bring me to one of the murderers.
Were he as strong as Hector, thus would I tear and drag
him up and down.   170

> *He beats the* Painter *in, the comes out again with a book*
> *in his hand.*

FIFTH ADDITION

(Replacing IV. iv. 168–90, but incorporating lines 176–8 and
168–75. See p. 126)

Castile. Why hast thou butchered both my children thus?

Hieronimo. But are you sure they are dead?

Castile.   Ay, slave, too sure.

Hieronimo. What, and yours too?

Viceroy. Ay, all are dead, not one of them survive.

Hieronimo. Nay, then I care not, come, and we shall be
friends;

   Let us lay our heads together.   5

   See, here's a goodly noose will hold them all.

Viceroy. O damnèd devil, how secure he is!

---

158. *Priam*] Tragic depictions of the fall of Troy to the Greeks were
common in Renaissance literature and art, as in *Hamlet*, II.ii, and *The Rape
of Lucrece*, 1366 ff., where the motif of *ecphrasis* is also pronounced (see n. 122
above).

167. *abuseth*] deceives.

169. *Hector*] mighty prince of Troy.

Fifth Addition

7. *secure*] arrogantly self-confident.

Hieronimo. Secure? Why dost thou wonder at it?
    I tell thee, Viceroy, this day I have seen revenge,
    And in that sight am grown a prouder monarch   10
    That ever sat under the crown of Spain.
    Had I as many lives as there be stars,
    As many heavens to go as those lives,
    I'd give them all, ay, and my soul to boot,
    But I would see thee ride in this red pool.   15
Castile. Speak, who were thy confederates in this?
Viceroy. That was thy daughter Bel-Imperia,
    For by her hand my Balthazar was slain.
    I saw her stab him.
Hieronimo.   O, good words!
    As dear to me was my Horatio   20
    As yours, or yours, or yours, my lord, to you.
    My guiltless son was by Lorenzo slain,
    And by Lorenzo and that Balthazar
    Am I at last revengèd thoroughly,
    Upon whose souls may heavens be yet revenged   25
    With greater far than these afflictions.
    Methinks since I grew inward with revenge
    I cannot look with scorn enough on death.
King. What, dost thou mock us, slave?—Bring tortures forth!
Hieronimo. Do, do, do, and meantime I'll torture you.   30
    You had a son, as I take it; and your son
    Should ha' been married to your daughter; ha, was 't not
        so?
    You had a son, too; he was my liege's nephew.
    He was proud and politic; had he lived,
    He might ha' come to wear the crown of Spain;   35
    I think 'twas so. 'Twas I that killèd him;
    Look you, this same hand, 'twas it that stabbed
    His heart—do you see this hand?—

12–14.] These lines are lifted, with variations, from Marlowe's *Doctor Faustus*, A-text, I.iii.104–5.
  15. *But I would see*] rather than not see.
  27. *inward*] intimate.
  31. *You*] the Viceroy of Portugal.
  32. *to your daughter*] to your (Castile's) daughter, Bel-imperia.
  33. *You had a son*] you (Castile) had a son (Lorenzo).

For one Horatio, if you ever knew him,
A youth, one that they hanged up in his father's garden,   40
One that did force your valiant son to yield,
While your more valiant son did take him prisoner.
Viceroy. Be deaf my senses; I can hear no more.
King. Fall, heaven, and cover us with thy sad ruins!
Castile. Roll and the world within thy pitchy cloud!   45
Hieronimo. Now do I applaud what I have acted.

Nunc iners cadat manus!

Now to express the rupture of my part,
First take my tongue, and afterwards my heart.
                                    He bites out his tongue.

---

41. *your valiant son*] your (the Viceroy's) valiant son, Balthazar.
42. *your more valiant son*] your (Castile's) more valiant son, Lorenzo.
47.] Now may my hand fall idle!

Further reading

The standard critical edition of Thomas Kyd is Frederick S. Boas, *The Works of Thomas Kyd* (Oxford, Clarendon Press, 1901). It is in old spelling, with textual collations and notes. Philip Edwards' edition of *The Spanish Tragedy* for the Revels Plays series (London: Methuen, and Cambridge, Mass.: Harvard University Press, 1959, reprinted in 1977 and subsequently by Manchester University Press) offers a comprehensive critical modern-spelling edition of this single play. More recent individual editions of *The Spanish Tragedy* include those of C. T. Prouty (New York: Crofts Classics, 1952), Thomas W. Ross (Fountainwell Drama Series, Berkeley: University of California Press, 1968), and J. R. Mulryne (Mermaid Dramabook, London: Benn, New York: Hill and Wang, 1970). Scolar Press (Leeds) published in 1966 a useful facsimile reprint of the original edition of the play. Andrew S. Cairncross's edition for the Regents Renaissance Drama Series (Lincoln: University of Nebraska Press, 1967) contains *The Spanish Tragedy* and *The First Part of Hieronimo*. The present edition is based on Philip Edwards' Revels edition.

Thomas Kyd's writings have not been as extensively analyzed in recent years as those of Shakespeare, Jonson, and Marlowe. Five book-length studies can be found in libraries: Philip Edwards, *Thomas Kyd and Early Elizabethan Tragedy* (London and New York: Longmans, Green, 1966); Arthur Friedman, *Thomas Kyd: Facts and Problems* (Oxford, Clarendon, 1967); Peter B. Murray, *Thomas Kyd* (New York: Twayne, 1969); Frank Ardolino, *Thomas Kyd's Mystery Play: Myth and Ritual in 'The Spanish Tragedy'* (New York: Peter Lang, 1985); and Ardolino, *Apocalypse and Armada in Kyd's 'Spanish Tragedy'* (Kirkville, Mo.: 16th-Century Journal Publishers, Northeast Missouri State U., 1995). Kyd is sometimes studied as a seminal figure in the larger dimension of Elizabethan revenge tragedy. Perhaps the most influential book in this regard is Fredson Bowers, *Elizabethan Revenge Tragedy, 1587–1642* (Princeton University Press, 1940). A similar context is to be found in Charles A. and Elaine S. Hallett, *The Revenger's Madness: A Study of Revenge Tragedy Motifs* (Lincoln: University of Nebraska Press, 1980), and in

Frederic Kiefer, *Fortune and Elizabethan Tragedy* (San Marino, Cal.: Huntington Library, 1983).

Kyd's influential play is the subject of serious attention in a number of book-length critical studies devoted to Renaissance tragedy and Renaissance drama. Joel B. Altman explores the function of rhetoric in *The Tudor Play of Mind: Rhetorical Inquiry and the Development of Elizabethan Drama* (Berkeley: University of California Press, 1978). Huston Diehl looks at the play-within-the-play in the context of Protestant–Catholic polemicism in *Staging Reform, Reforming the Stage: Protestantism and Popular Theater in Early Modern England* (Ithaca: Cornell University Press, 1997). Gordon Braden studies rhetorical frustration in relation to the larger shape of the revenge genre in *Renaissance Tragedy and the Senecan Tradition: Anger's Privilege* (New Haven: Yale University Press, 1985). C. L. Barber pursues a psychological reading in *Creating Elizabethan Tragedy: The Theater of Marlowe and Kyd*, edited by Richard P. Wheeler (University of Chicago Press, 1988).

Several useful collections of essays on the Elizabethan drama feature important essays on Kyd's play. George Hunter, 'Ironies of Justice in *The Spanish Tragedy*', first published in *Renaissance Drama* 8 (1965), 89–104, is included in *Shakespeare's·Contemporaries*, second edition, ed. Max Bluestone and Norman Rabkin (Englewood Cliffs, N.J.: Prentice-Hall, 1970). This collection also gives us Wolfgang Clemen on 'The Uses of Rhetoric', originally published in *English Tragedy before Shakespeare* (London: Methuen, 1961), and William K. Wiatt, 'The Dramatic Function of the Alexandro-Viluppo Episode in *The Spanish Tragedy*', originally appearing in *Notes and Queries* 5 (1958), 327–9. *Staging the Renaissance: Reinterpretations of Elizabethan and Jacobean Drama*, edited by David Scott Kastan and Peter Stallybrass (London and New York: Routledge, 1991), includes an original essay by James Shapiro on '"Tragedies naturally performed": Kyd's Representation of Violence, *The Spanish Tragedy* (c. 1587)'. S. F. Johnson, '*The Spanish Tragedy*: or, Babylon Revisited', appears in *Essays on Shakespeare and the Elizabethan Drama in Honor of Hardin Craig*, ed. Richard Hosley (Columbia: University of Missouri Press, 1962). Jonas A. Barish, '*The Spanish Tragedy*, or the Pleasure and Perils of Rhetoric', is printed in *Elizabethan Theatre*, ed. J. R. Brown and Bernard Harris, Studies-upon-Avon Studies 9 (London: E. Arnold, 1966).

Thematic studies of this play often focus on issues of revenge and violence. Geoffrey Aggeler, 'The Eschatological Crux in *The Spanish*

Tragedy', *JEGP* 86 (1987), 319–31, pays particular attention to questions of belief and judgement. See also Sacvan Berkovitch, 'Love and Strife in Kyd's *The Spanish Tragedy'*, *Studies in English Literature* 9 (1969), 215–29; David Laird, 'Hieronimo's Dilemma', *Studies in Philology* 62 (1965), 137–46; Michael Henry Levin, ' "Vindicta Mihi!" Meaning, Morality, and Motivation in *The Spanish Tragedy'*, *Studies in English Literature* 4 (1964), 307–24; Ernst de Chickera, 'Divine Justice and Private Revenge in *The Spanish Tragedy'*, *Modern Language Review* 57 (1962), 228–32; Margaret Scott, 'Machiavelli and Machiavelli', *Renaissance Drama* 15 (1984), 147–74; and Eugene D. Hill, 'Senecan and Vergilian Perspectives in *The Spanish Tragedy'*, *English Literary Renaissance* 15 (1985), 143–65. For a psychoanalytic approach to the play, see David P. Willburn, 'Thomas Kyd's *The Spanish Tragedy*: Inverted Vengeance', *American Imago'* 28 (1971), 247–67.

The language of violence and revenge is no less fascinating to critics. See, for example, Peter Sacks, ' "Where Words Prevail Not": Grief, Revenge, and Language in Kyd and Shakespeare', *ELH* 49 (1982), 576–601; Carol McGinnis Kay, 'Deception through Words: A Reading of *The Spanish Tragedy'*, *Studies in Philology* 74 (1977), 20–38; J. R. Mulryne, 'Nationality and Language in Thomas Kyd's *The Spanish Tragedy'*, in *Langues et nations au temps de la Renaissance*, ed. M. T. Jones-Davies (Paris: Klincksieck, 1991); and Scott McMillin, 'The Figure of Silence in *The Spanish Tragedy'*, *ELH* 39 (1972), 27–48.

Staging issues are explored in Sheldon P. Zitner, '*The Spanish Tragedy* and the Language of Performance', in *The Elizabethan Theatre XI*, ed. A. L. Magnussen and C. E. McGee (Port Credit, Ont.: P. D. Meany, 1990); Roslyn L. Knutson, 'Influence of the Repertory System on the Revival and Revision of *The Spanish Tragedy* and *Dr. Faustus'*, *English Literary Renaissance* 18 (1988), 257–74; James Siemon, 'Dialogical Formalism: Word, Object, and Action in *The Spanish Tragedy'*, *Medieval and Renaissance Drama in England* 5 (1991), 87–225; Eleanor M. Tweedie, ' "Action is Eloquence": The Staging of Thomas Kyd's *The Spanish Tragedy'*, *Studies in English Literature* 16 (1976), 233–9; and Donna B. Hamilton, '*The Spanish Tragedy*: A Speaking Picture', *English Literary Renaissance* 4 (1974), 203–17.